DESPERATE HOUSEWIVES OF BIBLICAL PROPORTIONS

MICHELLE P. JONES

**DESPERATE HOUSEWIVES
OF BIBLICAL PROPORTIONS**
Copyright © 2020 Michelle P. Jones
All rights reserved.

No part of this publication may be reproduced, transmitted, or stored in a retrieval system, in any form or by any means, electronic, mechanical, photocopying, recording or otherwise, without the prior permission of the author. This book of curriculum is sold subject to the condition that it shall not, by way of trade or otherwise, be lent, re-sold, hired or otherwise circulated without the author's prior consent/permission in any form of binding other than that in which it is published and without a similar condition including this condition being imposed on the subsequent purchaser.

Cover Created by Nicole Powell, NPinspired Design, LLC

Library of Congress Control Number: 2020918336
ISBN: 978-1-7351349-5-6

ACKNOWLEDGEMENTS

Thank You:
Nicole Powell, NPinspired Design, LLC, my graphic artist
Denola Burton, Enhanced DNA: Develop Nurture Achieve, LLC,
my publisher

A Special Thank You:
Jerry Brown and Tim Sullens for your invaluable contribution
to the creation of the summary. I thank God for bringing Godly
men into my inner circle to pour into me and to help guide me along
life's path!!!

DEDICATION

Throughout my life I have had giants in the Gospel who have taught me to go deeper in the Word of God to discover its mysteries and derive a greater and deeper understanding of God and the love He has for me. Teachers such as Elder Murph, Bishop James C. Hawkins, Evangelist Marva E. Bledsoe and Overseer Frederick Bradley, just to name a few, who have taught me. While writing this book, God assigned three (3) exceptional women to be my ears as they listened to different aspects of this literary project. Thank you for taking the time to listen, laugh, encourage and push me through this project. The Stilettos Consortium, you are a gift from God as my personal and Spiritual cheerleaders who have lovingly helped me see the vision, write the vision and make it plain so others can see it and run with it! May the blessings of God continue to rest, rule and abide in each of your lives. As I continue on this author's journey, I will continue to be eternally grateful for the blessing of each of you and the role you play in my life. Thank you for being the you I needed and for allowing me to use your ears and brains as these seven (7) matriarchs came to life on these pages while telling the story of the

Desperate Housewives of Biblical Proportions and their personal and/or Spiritual relationship with barrenness.

I love you to life!!!!

Blessings,

Michelle

ENDORSEMENTS

As a woman, wife, mother, and friend I connected on a deep level to Desperate Housewives of Biblical Proportions. The timing of this book is perfect for our times now but is also timeless because the stories are so relatable to what many women are faced with every day! In this world of highlight reels on social media it is easy for us to go about our lives and act as if everything is ok, when in reality it is not. I have found myself having thoughts of unworthiness and the story of Sarai, while talking about bareness, is a wonderful example and metaphor of how we as women can feel unworthy by not producing... x,y,z. An example is worth a thousand words. Using the 7 matriarchs of the Bible, Sarah, Hagar, Rebekah, Leah, Rachel, Bilhah and Zilpah, Michelle Jones helps her readers see how they can follow their examples in their daily lives. Buckle up! This would be a great book for a woman's study and I highly recommend it!

Melanie Fusilier
Parents Pursuing Purpose

In Michelle P. Jones' book, Desperate Housewives of Biblical Proportion, she makes the women of Genesis come alive. I feel like I know them more intimately and have a better understanding of their lives, their feelings, and their decisions. I highly recommend it to anyone who wants to learn more about Biblical women and how our lives today relate to what was written in the Bible.

Kelly Ekwurzel
Dynamic Clarity Coaching
Speaker, Trainer and Coach

This book delves into the many reasons why women in the Bible were constantly acting out of desperation. The history behind their actions is fascinating and educational. You will enjoy this book no matter your level of biblical history and knowledge.

Deb Hallberg, CEO
Pass the Torch for Women Foundation

I believe any woman who reads Desperate Housewives of Biblical Proportions will be able to identify with at least one of the stories from these inspiring women of the Bible. The trials each faced to live out God's purpose for their life, and the triumph they realized, will encourage, and enhance your growth as a woman of faith. If you are seeking fuel for your spiritual journey, this book is a must read!

Thresette Briggs
Chief Performance Officer
Performance 3

When God whispers to you about something bigger than yourself you must step fully into it just like Michelle P. Jones has done with this project. Michelle's personal and passionate beliefs about the Bible come to life as these characters overcome obstacles that we face in our everyday lives. This book is for anyone that has a hunger to learn the process of reflection and how to become stronger in your own spiritual journey.

Melahni Ake, Founder: Everyday Leaders
Everyday Leaders Daily Leadership Devotional

Michelle P. Jones takes biblical principles and breaks them down into digestible lessons in the Desperate Housewives of Biblical Proportions. Her insights make each lesson easy to understand and apply. She has taken some of my favorite women from the Bible and made them more relatable and she has introduced me to some lesser known women who I want to know better! This book is a must read!

Anza Goodbar
Life Design Strategist/Personal Development Coach

FOREWORD

By

Dr. Tuesday Tate
CEO, T. Tate Ministries International
CEO, ATK Speakers and Publishing Firm

I was struck by the reality and truth of the *"Desperate Housewives of Biblical Proportions,"* and how these seven (7) Matriarchs of Genesis are representative of the state of many women, today. The heart felt cry of being barren; of being without and unfulfilled is something way too many women are faced with. A greater challenge and truth is in how many may have suppressed the hurt, pain and even the reality of this truth. Often it is easier to say, "I'm good", "I'm fine", "It's ok, etc. when that isn't their reality at all. In the same way that the matriarchs in the *"Desperate Housewives of Biblical Proportions"* storyline is unlike the Bible story where Elisha had his servant ask the Shunammite woman if she was alright and her response to him was "Everything is alright" or "It is well'; though it wasn't. In this instance, her faith spoke those things that were not as though they were, unlike the matriarchs in the storyline. Too often Church lingo, like those I mentioned, are spoken with no sincerity nor faith but are spoken simply out of habit, expectation and/or tradition.

When a barren or empty heart is left unaddressed, the cry from and of the womb coupled with the pain in the heart will lead to desperation. Let me pause here and share what I mean by barren. Barren can represent an unfilled dream or desire, a loss suffered and never found that's lacking the hope or love needed to replace it, an unmet need and/or a longing. It is an emptiness that's brought on by something that's been left unsaid, undone and/or never resolved. This produces desperation... The word itself rings of someone being desperate. And, where there is desperation there's lack, scarcity, fear, doubt, unbelief and/or hopelessness. Through the message contained within the pages of this book, I pray you will find inspiration, motivation and revelation that empowers you to live! Jesus came, lived and died for you to have life and have or live it abundantly! I applaud Michelle for attacking such a layered topic, and how she has chosen to explore and unpack these seven (7) matriarchs of Genesis lives for your edification, will bless you.

Dr. Tuesday Tate
CEO, T. Tate Ministries International
CEO, ATK Speakers and Publishing Firm

TABLE OF CONTENTS

ACKNOWLEDGEMENTS	iii
DEDICATION	iv
ENDORSEMENTS	vi
FOREWORD	ix
INTRODUCTION	13
THE BIRTH OF A NATION	16
THE DESTRUCTIVENESS OF FAVORITISM	72
COMPARISON KILLS	103
CONCLUSION	147
BIBLIOGRAPHY	154

INTRODUCTION

The Desperate Housewives of Biblical Proportions story is based upon the television series, *Desperate Housewives*, and focuses on the four (4) housewives who hold the starring role in the series. The *Desperate Housewives* series uses dramatic comedy to display the domestic struggles and family life while the women face the challenges of keeping secrets, being front row witnesses to various crimes and mysteries hidden behind the front doors of their magnificent homes and in their beautiful and seemingly perfect lives. As has been said, *"everything that glitters ain't gold."*

During our journey called life every person has had an opportunity to act in desperation, however, not everyone makes the choice to act in that manner. Those that make the choice are acting from a place of hopelessness. A place where morality and integrity have taken a back seat to their desire to be successful in getting whatever seems to be their point of focus. As we get into our lesson, I want to make sure that we all are operationally defining our key words the same way:

DESPERATION (Desperate): A state of despair, typically one that results in rash or extreme behavior; wanting or needing something so badly that you will do anything, even if it's immoral, illegal, degrading, self-humiliating or in poor taste.

BARRENNESS: unable to produce; infertile; sterile; childless; empty of meaning or value; worthless; devoid of.

Throughout the character analysis of each woman that makes up the Desperate Housewives of Biblical Proportions, we find a common theme for them: *barrenness*. Barrenness at its most primal meaning is defined as being empty of meaning or value. This is significant because women throughout history have judged themselves negatively by what they couldn't do, didn't have and/or were unable to attain. They have determined their individual value by using the aforementioned standard, and for some reason have accepted this flawed way of thinking to justify their unworthiness and to support their low self-value or low self-esteem. A lot of the time we focus on the symptom not the bigger issue or the root cause. When I began this study, I thought I was sharing a significant and relevant Bible Story. What I did not see at the time is that it is so much more than that. In medicine, doctors find themselves treating the symptoms, the things we are concerned about, however, to find the root cause requires a different set of questions and an analysis of the information provided by the patient in conjunction with the tests results to come up with the root cause, the underlying reason for the symptoms presented.

The same is true of the seven (7) matriarchs in Genesis: Sarah, Hagar, Rebekah, Leah, Rachel, Bilhah and Zilpah. While looking at each of them individually and collectively, we can see that their condition is only a symptom of a bigger issue each are suffering through. Sometimes we have to look below the surface to really see what is going on. In this story, we find our matriarchs acting in desperation attempting to attain the thing they most desire without realizing that their act(s) of desperation speaks to how barrenness is playing out as well as infecting and affecting their life, their legacy and the direction and trajectory of an entire nation. Hopefully, as you take this journey with me you will see yourself, your symptoms, the underlying root cause of your issue while beginning to allow God's healing balm to heal your broken places as it empowers you to grow into the individual you are created, destined and purposed to be.

THE BIRTH OF A NATION
(Genesis 11:29-30; 12:4-18; -17; 13:14-18; 15:1-16:16; 21:1-21)

On these pages, discover how God's covenant relationships

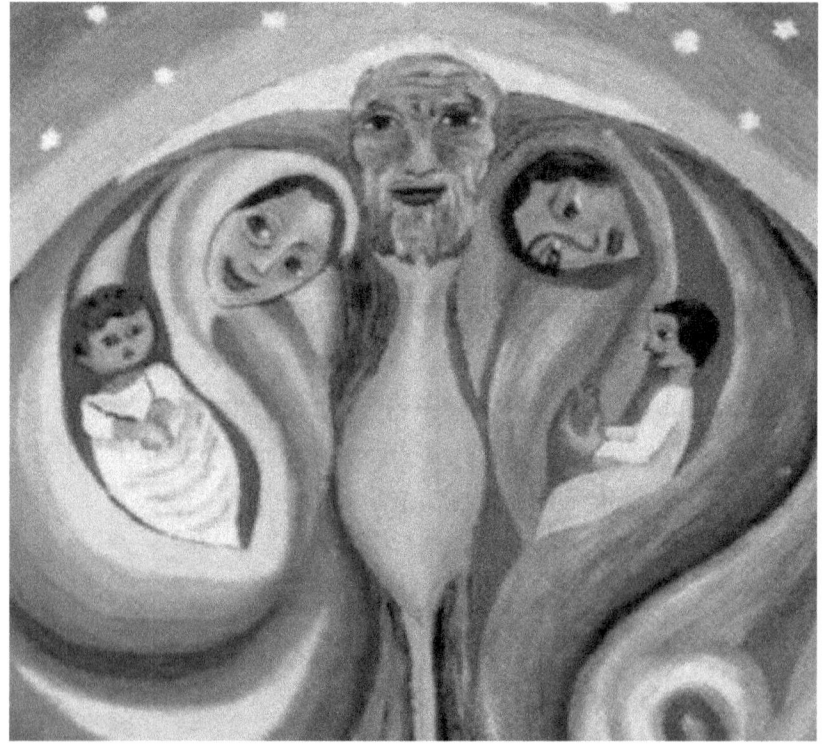

with Abraham, Hagar and Sarah leads to the birth of a nation.

SCRIPTURE LESSON: Genesis 11:29-30; 12:4-18; -17;

13:14-18; 15:1-16:16; 21:1-21)

GENESIS 11:²⁹ *And Abram and Nahor took them wives: the name of Abram's wife was Sarai; and the name of Nahor's wife, Milcah, the daughter of Haran, the father of Milcah, and the father of Iscah. ³⁰ But Sarai was barren; she had no child.*

GENESIS 12: *⁴ So Abram departed, as the* LORD *had spoken unto him; and Lot went with him: and Abram was seventy and five years old when he departed out of Haran. ⁵ And Abram took Sarai his wife, and Lot his brother's son, and all their substance that they had gathered, and the souls that they had gotten in Haran; and they went forth to go into the land of Canaan; and into the land of Canaan they came. ⁶ And Abram passed through the land unto the place of Sichem, unto the plain of Moreh. And the Canaanite was then in the land. ⁷ And the* LORD *appeared unto Abram, and said, Unto thy seed will I give this land: and there builded he an altar unto the* LORD, *who appeared unto him. ⁸ And he removed from thence unto a mountain on the east of Bethel, and pitched his tent, having Bethel on the west, and Hai on the east: and there he builded an altar unto the* LORD, *and called upon the name of the* LORD. *⁹ And Abram journeyed, going on still toward the south. ¹⁰ And there was a famine in the land: and Abram went down into Egypt to sojourn there; for the famine was grievous in the land. ¹¹ And it came to pass, when he was come near to enter into Egypt, that he said unto Sarai his wife, Behold now, I know that thou art a fair woman to look upon: ¹² Therefore it shall come to pass, when the Egyptians shall see thee, that they shall say, This is his wife: and they will kill me, but they will save thee alive. ¹³ Say, I pray thee, thou art my sister: that it may be well with me for thy sake; and my soul shall live because of thee. ¹⁴ And it came to pass, that, when*

Abram was come into Egypt, the Egyptians beheld the woman that she was very fair. ^{15} *The princes also of Pharaoh saw her and commended her before Pharaoh: and the woman was taken into Pharaoh's house.* ^{16} *And he entreated Abram well for her sake: and he had sheep, and oxen, and he asses, and menservants, and maidservants, and she asses, and camels.* ^{17} *And the* LORD *plagued Pharaoh and his house with great plagues because of Sarai Abram's wife.* ^{18} *And Pharaoh called Abram and said, what is this that thou hast done unto me? why didst thou not tell me that she was thy wife?*

GENESIS 13: ^{14} *And the* LORD *said unto Abram, after that Lot was separated from him, Lift up now thine eyes, and look from the place where thou art northward, and southward, and eastward, and westward:* ^{15} *For all the land which thou seest, to thee will I give it, and to thy seed forever.* ^{16} *And I will make thy seed as the dust of the earth: so that if a man can number the dust of the earth, then shall thy seed also be numbered.* ^{17} *Arise, walk through the land in the length of it and in the breadth of it; for I will give it unto thee.* ^{18} *Then Abram removed his tent, and came and dwelt in the plain of Mamre, which is in Hebron, and built there an altar unto the* LORD.

GENESIS 15: ^{1} *After these things the word of the* LORD *came unto Abram in a vision, saying, Fear not, Abram: I am thy shield, and thy exceeding great reward.* ^{2} *And Abram said,* LORD *God, what wilt thou give me, seeing I go childless, and the steward of my house is this Eliezer of Damascus?* ^{3} *And Abram said, Behold, to me thou hast given no seed: and, lo, one born in my house is mine heir.* ^{4} *And, behold, the word of the* LORD *came unto him, saying, This shall not be thine heir; but he that shall come forth out of thine own bowels shall be thine heir.* ^{5} *And he brought him forth abroad, and said, Look now toward* *heaven, and tell the stars, if thou be able to number them: and he said unto him, So shall thy seed be.* ⁶ *And he believed in the* LORD; *and he counted it to him for righteousness.* ⁷ *And he said unto him, I am the* LORD *that brought thee out of Ur of the Chaldees, to give thee this land to inherit it.* ⁸ *And he said,* LORD *God, whereby shall I know that I shall inherit it?* ⁹ *And he said unto him, Take me an heifer of three years old, and a she goat of three years old, and a ram of three years old, and a turtledove, and a young pigeon.* ¹⁰ *And he took unto him all these, and divided them in the midst, and laid each piece one against another: but the birds divided he not.* ¹¹ *And when the fowls came down upon the carcases, Abram drove them away.* ¹² *And when the sun was going down, a deep sleep fell upon Abram; and, lo, an horror of great darkness fell upon him.* ¹³ *And he said unto Abram, Know of a surety that thy seed shall be a stranger in a land that is not theirs, and shall serve them; and they shall afflict them four hundred years;* ¹⁴ *And also that nation, whom they shall serve, will I judge: and afterward shall they come out with great substance.* ¹⁵ *And thou shalt go to thy fathers in peace; thou shalt be buried in a good old age.* ¹⁶ *But in the fourth generation they shall come hither again: for the iniquity of the Amorites is not yet full.* ¹⁷ *And it came to pass, that, when the sun went down, and it was dark, behold a smoking furnace, and a burning lamp that passed between those pieces.* ¹⁸ *In the same day the* LORD *made a covenant with Abram, saying, Unto thy seed have I given this land, from the river of Egypt unto the great river, the river Euphrates:* ¹⁹ *The Kenites, and the Kenizzites, and the Kadmonites,* ²⁰ *And the Hittites, and the Perizzites, and the Rephaims,* ²¹ *And the Amorites, and the Canaanites, and the Girgashites, and the Jebusites.*

GENESIS 16: *¹Now Sarai Abram's wife bare him no children: and she had an handmaid, an Egyptian, whose name was Hagar. ² And Sarai said unto Abram, Behold now, the* LORD *hath restrained me from bearing: I pray thee, go in unto my maid; it may be that I may obtain children by her. And Abram hearkened to the voice of Sarai. ³ And Sarai Abram's wife took Hagar her maid the Egyptian, after Abram had dwelt ten years in the land of Canaan and gave her to her husband Abram to be his wife. ⁴ And he went in unto Hagar, and she conceived: and when she saw that she had conceived, her mistress was despised in her eyes. ⁵ And Sarai said unto Abram, My wrong be upon thee: I have given my maid into thy bosom; and when she saw that she had conceived, I was despised in her eyes: the* LORD *judge between me and thee. ⁶ But Abram said unto Sarai, Behold, thy maid is in thine hand; do to her as it pleaseth thee. And when Sarai dealt hardly with her, she fled from her face. ⁷ And the angel of the* LORD *found her by a fountain of water in the wilderness, by the fountain in the way to Shur. ⁸ And he said, Hagar, Sarai's maid, whence camest thou? and whither wilt thou go? And she said, I flee from the face of my mistress Sarai. ⁹ And the angel of the* LORD *said unto her, Return to thy mistress, and submit thyself under her hands. ¹⁰ And the angel of the* LORD *said unto her, I will multiply thy seed exceedingly, that it shall not be numbered for multitude. ¹¹ And the angel of the* LORD *said unto her, Behold, thou art with child and shalt bear a son, and shalt call his name Ishmael; because the* LORD *hath heard thy affliction. ¹² And he will be a wild man; his hand will be against every man, and every man's hand against him; and he shall dwell in the presence of all his brethren. ¹³ And she called the name of the* LORD *that spake unto her, Thou God seest me: for she said, Have I also here looked after him that seeth me? ¹⁴ Wherefore the well was* called Beerlahairoi; behold, it is between Kadesh and Bered. ¹⁵ And Hagar bare Abram a son: and Abram called his son's name, which Hagar bare, Ishmael. ¹⁶ And Abram was fourscore and six years old, when Hagar bare Ishmael to Abram.

GENESIS 21 ¹And the LORD visited Sarah as he had said, and the LORD did unto Sarah as he had spoken. ²For Sarah conceived, and bare Abraham a son in his old age, at the set time of which God had spoken to him. ³And Abraham called the name of his son that was born unto him, whom Sarah bare to him, Isaac. ⁴And Abraham circumcised his son Isaac being eight days old, as God had commanded him. ⁵And Abraham was an hundred years old, when his son Isaac was born unto him. ⁶And Sarah said, God hath made me to laugh, so that all that hear will laugh with me. ⁷And she said, Who would have said unto Abraham, that Sarah should have given children suck? for I have born him a son in his old age. ⁸And the child grew and was weaned: and Abraham made a great feast the same day that Isaac was weaned. ⁹And Sarah saw the son of Hagar the Egyptian, which she had born unto Abraham, mocking. ¹⁰Wherefore she said unto Abraham, Cast out this bondwoman and her son: for the son of this bondwoman shall not be heir with my son, even with Isaac. ¹¹And the thing was very grievous in Abraham's sight because of his son. ¹²And God said unto Abraham, Let it not be grievous in thy sight because of the lad, and because of thy bondwoman; in all that Sarah hath said unto thee, hearken unto her voice; for in Isaac shall thy seed be called. ¹³And also of the son of the bondwoman will I make a nation, because he is thy seed. ¹⁴And Abraham rose up early in the morning, and took bread, and a bottle of water, and gave it unto Hagar, putting it on her shoulder, and the child, and sent her away: and she departed, and *wandered in the wilderness of Beersheba.* ¹⁵ *And the water was spent in the bottle, and she cast the child under one of the shrubs.* ¹⁶ *And she went, and sat her down over against him a good way off, as it were a bow shot: for she said, Let me not see the death of the child. And she sat over against him, and lift up her voice, and wept.* ¹⁷ *And God heard the voice of the lad; and the angel of God called to Hagar out of heaven, and said unto her, What aileth thee, Hagar? fear not; for God hath heard the voice of the lad where he is.* ¹⁸ *Arise, lift up the lad, and hold him in thine hand; for I will make him a great nation.* ¹⁹ *And God opened her eyes, and she saw a well of water; and she went, and filled the bottle with water, and gave the lad drink.* ²⁰ *And God was with the lad; and he grew, and dwelt in the wilderness, and became an archer.* ²¹ *And he dwelt in the wilderness of Paran: and his mother took him a wife out of the land of Egypt.*

INTRODUCTION

When God began to speak into the heart and mind of man, He chose men whose hearts were already turned towards Him and following His lead wasn't a decision but an action waiting to happen. One such man is Abram (Abraham). We see our Patriarch make his grand entrance in Genesis 11:29 when he is choosing Sarai as a wife. Life as they knew it ceased to exist when God spoke to Abram and told him to *"Leave your country, your people and your father's household and go to the land I will show you."* The conversation that God has with Abram is full of promise (and is the beginning of the 4th Dispensation: Promise, Genesis 12:1 – Exodus 18:27). Abram did as God instructed and took with him his wife, Sarai, his nephew, Lot, his family and all the possessions they had accumulated and the people he had acquired as they sojourned to Canaan (Genesis 12:4-5).

BARRENNESS: Throughout time women have been unable to produce children or are infertile. During the day and time that Sarai lived it was believed that being infertile or barren was God showing His displeasure with the woman. A woman's status within the family unit and the community was based upon and/or identified by her ability to have children, specifically male children. In Genesis 11:30, we learn that Sarai is barren. According to the Britannica Encyclopedia, Sarai's barrenness shows forth the tension that plagues Abram's household and becomes a central theme of Sarai's storyline in our lesson on the Desperate Housewives of Biblical Proportions. In Sarai's eyes, her condition doesn't seem to speak clearly of God's promise to make Abram the Patriarch and founder of a great nation. Here we find Sarai focused on her condition and not God's promises. Simply put she focused on fact instead of having faith!

According to the Jewish Virtual Library, children are the greatest blessing: *"a heritage of the Lord"* (Psalm 127:3-5), and that procreation is one of the main purposes of marriage. It was often believed that an offspring (especially a male offspring) was prized because it meant that Kaddish would be recited in one's memory. Within the Jewish community, barrenness is viewed as a curse and a punishment (Leviticus 20:20-21; Jeremiah 22:30) and the cause of the shame placed upon the childless wife. The Midrash fully acknowledged the domestic suffering of childless women: even if the barren wife had no religious obligations to fulfill, she is believed to have failed to fulfill the primary expectation of her social role, since *"it is children who assure a wife's position in her home."* In my studies, I learned that it is an acceptable Jewish tradition for a husband to divorce his wife after ten (10) years of infertility. Some men in a childless marriage choose to take a second wife rather than divorce an apparently infertile spouse. Aggadah text generally deplored the dissolution of marriages, even when male procreation is at stake, honoring the preservation of a loving childless marriage as a solution where human needs and feelings overrule legal prescriptions.

TIMING. In today's vernacular we often say that *"God's delay isn't His denial."* However, when we are experiencing it the understanding alludes us leaving us concerned and if we want to be honest it leaves us depressed and desperate to have that thing that seems to be just out of our reach. The challenges both Abram and Sarai face as they continue to follow and believe in a God who makes promises that aren't immediately realized, speaks to each of us when we must believe and have faith that God will perform His promises even when we cannot see it. Think about it in the same way as, a child waiting for Christmas morning. Anxious to see what Santa has left him/her under the tree. The closer they get to Christmas morning the higher the anxiety. The more the anticipation sets in and magnifies their expectations and their guessing of what the child will get. Now think about Sarai! At least the child knew when they'd get their present(s), however, Sarai has no clue when the promised seed would be given to her and the promised child would be conceived. Every day it didn't happen had to be difficult and spoke more and more to the fact that there would be a point of no return for Sarai as her body prepares to go through menopause, and there's no conception, no pregnancy and no birth!

When Abram and Sarai first started their journey, they were

75 and 65 years of age, respectfully. The Bible clearly specifies Abram and Sarai's age for a reason, and clearly shows that Abraham fathered, and Sarah conceived a child in their old age. One of the things that became apparent to me is that there was a 39 year span from Promise to performance. Why? Some say that God was strengthening Abram's faith and preparing him for his promised role as the patriarch of the entire (Jewish) Israelite nation. During that time Abram, with Sarai by his side, built relationships, fought for God's people and began to create a legacy. (Lamentations 3:16 says, *"…it is good to wait quietly for the salvation of the Lord."* Psalms 37:7 says, *"Be still before the Lord and wait patiently for him…"*) The journey Abram and Sarai took physically, mentally and Spiritually to enter into the promises God had for them played out daily in their lives. It wasn't designed to depress or cause them to act in desperation; it was meant to prepare them for the actualization of the promise. Peter 3:8-9 says, *"But do not forget one thing, dear friends; with the Lord a day is like a thousand years, and a thousand years are like one day. The Lord is not slow in keeping His promise, as some understand slowness."* (Reference Scriptures: Ecclesiastes 3:1-8; Ecclesiastes 3:11; Acts 1:7; Galatians 4:4)

According to *www.Pathos.com*, *"Top 7 Bible Verses About God's Timing"* by Jada Pryor, June 26, 2015, *"Sometimes it seems as if we are not even on God's clock. Yet, there is never a time in which He is not aware of the desires of our hearts. He does, however, know better than we do, whether what we want to happen, is necessary or good for us. Sometimes His timing may be just the amount of time we need to see that what we thought we needed, we never did or that the waiting made the receiving that much better. His timing will always be perfect, even when our trust in it is not… in a relationship with God …your patience is always rewarded. It may not have fit your timetable or schedule, and it may not look the way you thought it would, but it will come exactly when it was supposed to …right on time."*

HAGAR (ISHMAEL)

Hagar is an Ancient Egyptian handmaiden to Sarah. It is believed by some theologians that Hagar was a gift given to Sarai during her stay in the Pharaoh's palace as a part of the gifts bestowed upon her as an intended wife to the Pharaoh, and a part of the Pharaoh's harem. When Sarai was returned to Abram, all the gifts remained with Abram and Sarai (Genesis 12:14-20). After ten (10) years of a childless marriage, Sarai gives her handmaid, Hagar, to Abram in an attempt to ensure the Abrahamic Covenant is fulfilled. Abram agrees and Hagar conceives, and Ishmael is born as a result of their union. Sarai complained during Hagar's pregnancy that Hagar no longer respected her which led to Sarai's mistreatment of Hagar. In Genesis 15:5, Sarai says to Abram, "…*My wrong be upon thee; I have given my maid into thy bosom; and when she saw that she had conceived, I was despised in her eyes…*" Abram replies, "…*thy maid is in thy hand; do to her as it pleaseth thee.*" (Genesis 15:6). In response to Abram's reply Sarai begins to treat Hagar harshly, and because of Sarai's mistreatment Hagar runs away. While on the run, Hagar has an encounter with "…*an angel of the Lord…*" who encourages her to return and "…*submit thyself under her hands.*" (Genesis 16:3). After Hagar returns to Abram's household and submits herself to Sarai, Hagar gives birth to a son. Abram names the son, **Ishmael** (*God will hear*). This is an important caveat in Hagar's story.

Abram names the child instead of Sarai which goes against the custom of the land and against the reason for Sarai offering her maid, Hagar, to Abram. Hagar was to act as a surrogate and any child she birthed would become Sarai's child. It is also noteworthy that Abram is 86 years old when Ishmael is born.

When Ishmael was 13, he, Abram and all the males within the household were circumcised as a part of the Abrahamic covenant. At age 14, Hagar and Ishmael were expelled from Abraham's household at Sarah's request. Sarah tells Abraham in Genesis 21:10, "*…Cast out this bondwoman and her son: for the son of this bondwoman shall not be heir with my son…*" Abraham's love for Ishmael caused him to be deeply grieved at Sarah's request until God told him "*in Isaac your seed shall be called,*" and a great nation would come from Ishmael because of him being his son (Genesis 21:11-12; 17:18-21). After their expulsion, Hagar and Ishmael run out of food and water, and Hagar sits Ishmael some distance away from her so she wouldn't have to see him die. That's when she has an encounter with God who saves them alive and assures Hagar that Ismael will be the forefather of a great nation. God was with the lad; and he grew and dwelt in the wilderness and became an archer (Genesis 21:14-21). When Hagar determined it was time for Ishmael to marry, she found him a wife from the land of Egypt. The marriage produced twelve (12) sons who became tribal chiefs throughout the regions of Havilah to Shur (from Assyria to Egypt). Ishmael also had one daughter Mahalath

(Basemoth) who later became Esau's third wife. Upon Abraham's death Ishmael and Isaac buried him in the Cave of the Patriarchs with his beloved Sarah. Ishmael later died at the age of 137.

PARENTHETICAL CITATION: Ishmael is recognized as an important prophet and patriarch of Islam. Muslims believe that Ishmael is the ancestor of several prominent Arab tribes and the forefather of Muhammad and that Muhammad was the descendant of Ishmael who would establish a great nation, as promised by God. Scholars believe the Muslims by way of the Arabs is the great nation God spoke to both Abraham and Hagar that would come from Ishmael.

HUMILITY: Let's take a deeper dive into Genesis 16:1-15 to discover Hagar's relationship with barrenness. In the scripture lesson, we find Sarai complaining that Hagar no longer respects her nor the authority she has in and over her life as her mistress. Abram replies to Sarai's complaint to "*…do unto her as it pleaseth thee…*" That was all the permission that Sarai needed to mistreat Hagar. Her mistreatment resulted in Hagar running away from Sarai and into an encounter with God that taught her a lesson in humility that would be God's first step in preparing Hagar to birth a nation. During her encounter with God, she's told

1. Return to your mistress
2. Submit yourself to your mistress
3. God hears, He knows, and He sees you
4. God offers stability in adversarial situations

5. God blesses in the face of hostility

Hagar returns as instructed and births Abram's first son, Ishmael, and continued to submit to Sarai until she is cast out of the camp with her son to have a desert experience with God. Think about it for a minute, for 14 years Hagar submitted to Sarah's rule over her and learned the difference between humility and humiliation.

HUMILITY: the quality of being humble; a modest opinion or estimate of one's own importance, rank, etc.

HUMILIATION: a strong feeling of embarrassment or mortification; the shame one feels when someone makes them appear stupid or when they make a mistake.

Although scripture does not support it, I am sure at various times during those 14 years Hagar did feel humiliated, however, she remembered what God had instructed and continued to submit to Sarah. Without realizing it Hagar became a living example of Colossians 3:23-24 KJV *"And whatsoever ye do, do it heartily, as to the Lord, and not unto men; knowing that of the Lord ye shall receive the reward of the inheritance for ye serve the Lord Christ."* From Hagar we find the following takeaways to apply to our own lives:

1. Don't run away when faced with adversarial treatment (if you did, go back)
2. Submit yourself to those who have rule over you
3. Handle hostility with love
4. Keep moving, living, loving and speaking for God

5. Know that God sees you, He hears you and He knows all that you have endured and/or is going through.

In God's original instructions to Abram in Genesis 12:1-3 He says, "*...and I will bless those who bless you; and the one who curses you, I will curse.*" This is played out numerous times while Abram goes on this journey with God. One (1) specific time we see this is when Hagar submits herself to Sarai as instructed by God. The covenant relationship that Hagar enters into with God turns out to be a double blessing. The first being the blessing of protection God provides for Hagar when she ran away from Sarai's verbal, mental and emotional abuse. The second being the blessing of provision God provides for Hagar and Ishmael when they are cast out of Abram's camp, family and life at the insistence of Sarai. This is significant because it is an illustration of how God protects and provides for those, He is in covenant relationship with and their seed. Without even realizing it, Hagar became a part of the blessings God promises from her willingness to be a surrogate to Sarah, her willingness to follow God's instructions to return and her willingness to submit as God taught her how to conduct herself in the face of adversity and the importance of practicing humility. The challenges Hagar faced and the humiliation she endured prepared her to one (1) day be the matriarch of a great nation and included in the sacred writings as one (1) of the seven (7) matriarchs spoken of in the book of Genesis.

IMAGE/LIKENESS: In Genesis 1:26 man is described as "*...made in the image and likeness of God.*" While thinking on this, I realized the significance of the scripture in the lives of the matriarchs of Genesis. To ensure we are operating from the same foundational truths, I will operationally define the two (2) key words from Genesis 1:26 image and likeness:

Image: (Tselem) a masculine noun meaning a likeness, a statue, a model, a drawing; a shadow.

Likeness: (Dmuwth) a feminine noun; this word is used to describe a human being as being created in the image or likeness of God.

As mankind is made in the image and likeness of God they also operate or rather have the ability to operate Spiritually in the same way that God does in the beginning chapters of the book of Genesis. Growing up in Church, I was often told that "...*life and death is in the power of the tongue.*" (Proverbs 18:21). The relevance of that scripture began to speak to the significance of Genesis 1:26 and the entire creation story. God spoke into the abyss and created all of creation in the same way that He spoke into the abyss of barrenness in not only Hagar's life, but all the women identified as the seven (7) matriarchs of Genesis. God spoke to Hagar through the angel at one (1) of her most vulnerable and low points of her life. He spoke hope into and over her life (situation) and that of her unborn son. Those words entered into her ear canal and traveled directly to the place of hurt within her and reverberated hope, love, understanding and acceptance. In that one (1) conversation, she received everything her heart, mind and soul needed to continue moving forward.

It gave her the courage, strength and the power to put one foot in front of the other and return to her place of humiliation, hurt and degradation while understanding her purpose and to accept her state while honoring Abraham's God of purpose who looked past her facade, her boastful words, built up walls of protection and shame, and saw her at the very core of her being: a woman created in the very image and likeness of God. With that in mind, she knew she'd endure. We have no doubt that she endured and did so with wisdom and grace. Hagar's actions, belief and newfound purpose set the scene that created the foundation that Job stood on when faced with loss, hurt and adversity in Job 41:1 where Job concedes to the power and majesty of God. *"Then Job answered the Lord and said, I know that thou canst do everything, and no thought can be withholden from thee."*

There is so much to learn from Hagar's role as a matriarch in Genesis that has gone unsaid and unexplained. It is as if Hagar's testimony shows us our limited capacity to understand our purpose or even realize it, for that matter. Hagar's testimony and life after her encounter speaks to Isaiah 55:9 and her realization that she is developing an intimate relationship with a God whose *"…ways are higher than your ways and… thoughts than your thoughts."* As we take a glimpse into the newly developing relationship Hagar has with God, He reveals Himself to her in the same way He desires to reveal Himself to all of mankind. I am sure there were Job-like moments in Hagar's life during those fourteen years where she had to have encouraging and reaffirming conversation(s) with God to remind her of His promises in the same way He speaks to His children today through Jeremiah 29:11, *"For I know the thoughts I think toward you saith the Lord, thoughts of peace and not evil to give you an expected end."* The challenge that every Christian experiences here is that we stop short of the promises found if we would only keep reading Jeremiah 29:12-14, *"Then shall ye call upon me, and ye shall go and pray unto me; and I will hearken unto you. And ye shall seek me, and find me, when ye shall search for me with all your heart. And I will be found of you, saith the Lord; and I will turn away your captivity and I will gather you from all nations and from all the places whither I have driven you, saith the Lord; and I will bring you again into the place whence I caused you to be carried away captive."*

Think about everything you have learned about Hagar and consider how God used her and her testimony for many of the Bible characters to find themselves standing on the foundation Hagar built when God spoke into and over her life during two (2) pivotal moments in her life, her destiny and her relationship with God. Hagar couldn't see it, but God was preparing her to raise the very child of promise God tells her about in Genesis 16:9-12 after their expulsion. Simply put, her submission to Sarai opened the door for God to teach her humility as God prepares her to continue raising her son as a single mother while facing the challenges they would encounter because of his personality and the path his life would take as he grew into the man God created, designed, destined and purposed him to be. I thank God that her story did not end in the desert but came alive as an entire nation was given what it needed to be birthed. That same nation that is at odds with the Israelite nation today which is evident in their continuous fight over their doctrinal beliefs, land and their place in history.

BREAKING POINT: As I was listening to Sarah Jakes Roberts' sermon entitled *"Breaking Point"* (1 Samuel 1:4-11), God began to speak to me regarding Hagar, when she said *"…come up to the tabernacle in the place that marks the spot where she is to meet God…"* and it made me put pen to paper to disclose that Hannah wasn't the only woman who had reached her breaking point. Hagar had reached her breaking point and is the reason she ran away from her abuser *"…to the place that marks the spot where she is to meet God…"* Think about it for a moment. Hagar unknowingly runs to the place that marks the spot where she is to meet God and have a life changing experience that quite literally prepares her to birth a nation. In that one (1) act, Hagar runs *"…to the place that marks the spot…"* where destiny meets up with reality in her life. Hagar's placement as Sarai's handmaid wasn't by chance but was a destiny move on God's part. A move that positioned her to experience her breaking point which directly resulted in her running *"…to the place that marks the spot where she meets God…"*, discovers her purpose, begins her preparation to birth a nation, her relationship with barrenness is identified and addressed and she becomes legacy minded. As she submitted to God's instructions she was stepping into her destiny, purpose and the promises of God. I am inclined to mention that when Hagar submits (yields to the will of another person) to both Sarai and God, she doesn't lose who she is, nor does she cease to exist as a free moral agent. Hagar simply makes the choice to submit and God honors her choice.

The many facets of Hagar's life, motherhood and legacy were birthed and encouraged to grow when Hagar had that private moment with God's emissary as God used him to speak into and over Hagar's life. That one (1) encounter gave her life purpose, direction and acceptance. Many women today are looking for acceptance in all the wrong places. When in reality all they have to do is accept Jesus Christ as their personal Lord and Savior and position themselves as Hagar did by submitting to give God the opportunity to speak into and over their lives and experience what Hagar did: the realization that God truly sees, cares and is waiting to speak love into the hurt places and see you! Really see you to the point where that one look and acknowledgement heals all the hurt and broken places within and allows wholeness to happen in your life. God desires for you to come to "*…the place that marks the spot where you are to meet God 'while allowing Him to speak…*" directly to your personal relationship with barrenness.

LET'S TALK ABOUT IT. In what ways are you able to relate to Hagar's story? In this season, how is God trying to show up in your life? Have you identified your personal relationship with barrenness that God is waiting to heal?

BIBLE GUIDE QUESTIONS:

1. Who is Hagar?

   _____

   _____

   _____

   _____

2. What does Ishmael's name mean? How does Ishmael's name speak to Hagar's purpose?

   _____

   _____

   _____

   _____

3. In your own words, describe the Hagaric Covenant and its relevance in the life of Christian women today?

   _____

   _____

4. Describe Hagar's relationship with barrenness and how God dealt with her regarding it?

5. In your own words define barrenness and why women throughout history have a relationship with it?

SARAI/SARAH

(princess)

The circumstances, customs and beliefs of the day created the perfect storm in which Sarai lived. Having no say in how they lived other than how her home operated, begins our story of how Sarai was renamed Sarah and became the matriarch of the nation of Israel. When Abram acted upon the promises of God it changed the dynamic in which he and his family lived. They went from being stationary camp dwellers to being nomads. Moving often with a specific destination in mind or so it seemed.

NOMAD: a person with no settled home; moving from place to place as a way of obtaining food, finding pasture for livestock or otherwise making a living.

The interesting thing here is that Abram believed God and as a result his wife followed his direction. Sarai wanted for Abram the promises God made, and for herself she desired a child, specifically a male child. That one (1) thing had the potential of cementing her place within the family and removing the curse and shame of barrenness from her life, her marriage and her home. It also had the ability to make her accepted amongst her peers. The challenges she faced, the secrets she kept and the humiliation she experienced while on this journey to fulfillment is worth it, if or rather when Sarai receives the promised seed, conceives and births the progenitor of the nation of Israel.

PROGENITOR: a person or thing from which a person, animal or plant is descended or originates; an ancestor or parent.

To better understand Sarai, let's take a quick look at Abram. Abram is the son of Terah, there is no mention of his mother. He has two (2) brothers Haran and Nahor, and has one (1) nephew, Lot, who travels with him for a while. According to the scriptures, Abram hears from God and packs up his family, his belongings and follows God's instructions to leave his father's house and journey to a land that He will show him (Genesis 12:1), and with no other instructions, only promises, we find Abram doing as instructed. In Abram's immediate obedience to God's instructions, we find a man who desires more and realizes for his existence to have greater meaning and for his legacy to span generations, his obedience is necessary. When God spoke to Abram, He didn't give him his final destination but promised to reward his obedience with directions, instructions, favor, blessings and a personal relationship. This is implied in Genesis 12:1 where God says "...*unto a land that I will shew thee.*" If Abram's personality, mentality and blind faith is any indication, then Sarai has a comparable personality and drive.

PARENTHETICAL CITATION: Abram is said to be the patriarch of Judaism, Christianity and Islam. In Judaism, he is the founding father of the Covenant of Pieces, the special relationship between the Hebrews and God; in Christianity he is the prototype of all believers, Jewish and Gentile alike; and in Islam he is seen as a link in the chain of prophets that begins with Adam and culminates in Muhammad.

Let me not get ahead of myself, let's begin a Biblical character analysis of Sarai when Abram leaves family and country to receive the promises of God.

LAW OF ATTRACTION: The Law of Attraction states, "*…that people and their thoughts are made from "pure energy," and that a process of like energy attracting like energy exists…*" (Wikipedia). If this is to be believed, then when Abram chose Sarai, he was choosing someone who was like-minded and understood his need and desire to follow after God and to benefit from His promises without realizing it. Sarai follows Abram's lead, and goes on a journey of fulfillment, purpose and promise. What isn't said, but implied is that when God calls Abram and by default Sarai, He does so with their personality, character and morality intact. It is while on this journey that God begins to change what is into what needs to be to ensure they're prepared for the realization or the actualization of the promises given by God. Everything that happens while Abram and Sarai take this journey is necessary to ensure the promised seed is raised up in the admonition of God.

Just like in our own Christian lives, the destination is only as important or significant as the journey the Christian takes to get there. While on this journey, as Sarai follows Abram it required her to be a willing participant to Abram's omissions that can really be seen as his deceptions. One such omission is when Abram tells Sarai not to tell the Pharaoh or his men that she's his wife for fear that they will kill him in order to have her. Sarai is described as beautiful and pleasing to look upon. So much so, that Abram knew Pharaoh would want her to be a part of his harem. As luck would have it, Sarai is believed to only be Abram's half-sister and not his wife. In His own unique way, God informs Pharaoh of Abram's omission and the Pharaoh sends Abram on his way with all his possessions, his wife and the gifts he received from Pharaoh for Sarai, intact. One of those gifts is a handmaid, Hagar, that was gifted to Sarai as an intended wedding present from the Pharaoh. This same scenario happens again in Genesis 20:1-20, where Abraham tells King Abimelech that Sarah is his sister and fails to also share that she is his wife. God intervenes here and informs the King that Sarah is a married woman. King Abimelech returns Sarah to Abraham untouched and blesses him with cattle, slaves, silver and permission for them to live wherever they like. As a result of Abraham's omission, God closed up every womb in Abimelech's household from the time of Sarah's taking until Abraham prayed to God.

Think about it for a minute! How would Sarah have acted had she believed Abraham was the barren one? Would she have used the opportunities presented from Abraham's omissions to become pregnant to have what she most desired: a child? How would her actions have affected the promises God had given to Abraham? I asked myself while studying this, *"is this the reason why God sent plagues to infect Pharaoh and his people and why God shut up the reproductive processes in King Abimelech and his people?"*

Throughout Genesis we find women acting contrary to the instructions and promises given to the men who are in relationship/communication with God in an attempt to help. Consider Eve's actions in the Garden of Eden and Sarah's actions in her character analysis, and how they speak to each woman's relationship with barrenness. I challenge and encourage you to take this journey with me as we take a deep dive into Sarai's life, actions, her relationship with barrenness and her commitment to support her husband, and how God uses perfectly flawed people to do extraordinary things that align with His perfect will.

HISTORICAL ANALYSIS: Sarai is the daughter of Terah and her mother (although different than Abram's) remains unnamed in the history books. Sarai's name is the feminine form of Sar meaning "chieftain" or "prince." Sarai marries Abram sometime between the ages of 40 and 45 and soon thereafter leaves everything she knows to go on this journey of promise, performance and prosperity with Abram.

PARENTHETICAL CITATION: Some theologians surmise that Abram publicly humiliated Nimrod, the king of Shinar (Mesopotamia) in his efforts to proclaim himself a god. He sought to destroy Abram because of Abram's public unwillingness to accept and support Nimrod's claims. (Wikipedia)

Let's not take lightly the journey Sarai took with her husband, Abram. It was on this journey that Sarai lost things that were only meant to travel a short distance with her and gained things that have been her lifelong companions. Just like with us today, people, situations and/or circumstances are in our life for a moment, a season or a lifetime. It is our responsibility to determine why they are there, dismiss them upon their expiration date and take with us the impact and the impression they left upon our life, heart and mind. The tools acquired and the information obtained all are necessary as we continue on our journey to self-awareness, self-enlightenment, a personal relationship with God and our willingness and ability to discover, accept and live our purpose OUT LOUD and in living color.

We pick up our storyline with Sarai making a unilateral decision to help God make His promise to her husband, Abram, a reality. Sarai couldn't imagine herself becoming pregnant the older she got and the more her childbearing years were passing her by. Now remember she left home and country to take this journey but did not leave or divorce herself from the influence the customs of the day had upon her, her life and her beliefs. With that being said, Sarai relies upon one of those customs/beliefs to help God out. The Assyrian Tablet contains the Assyrian marriage contracts which are the earliest known prenuptial agreements in the world and makes the first known reference to infertility. It stipulates that if the couple cannot produce a child within the first two (2) years of marriage, they will appoint a female slave as a surrogate. The woman, known as a ***hierodule***, would be freed from slavery after the birth of a son, and it has provisions to guard against polygamy and divorce specifying that the husband may not take another wife and if either of them choose to divorce the other, they will have to pay a specified fee. It is believed that these crude surrogacy arrangements were widespread in ancient Mesopotamia and Egypt. The first surrogate described in the Bible was Hagar when Sarai offers her to Abram.

LEFT BEHIND

In Genesis 16:1-4, we find Sarai offering Hagar to Abram in an attempt to help God bring His promise to Abram to fulfillment. Think about this for a minute! Does the God you serve need your assistance or permission to bring His promises to fulfillment, other than total obedience and acceptance of God's will in and over your life? One of the challenges Sarai faced is having to leave everything behind to take this journey. She was forced to stop being who she was and become the woman God created, destined and purposed her to be. She was challenged with leaving her idealisms, customs and her overall lifestyle behind. What most fail to see is that even though she was childless, she had created a life and home around her barrenness. (It's amazing how we can live around instead of in spite of our circumstances.) Keep in mind we are talking about a woman who went from a stationary home to a nomad lifestyle.

I am sure with the magnitude of the move there was a lot of planning and coordinating of resources to ensure the journey would be uneventful and successful. The question I must ask is how can you plan a lifestyle change? A lifestyle that changes you from being concerned about one home to being legacy minded. It is the same when a Christian begins their journey to a deeper more intimate relationship with Jesus Christ. It has become abundantly clear to me that God has instructed us to "*…let this mind be in you, which is also in Christ Jesus.*" (Philippians 2:5) Before any journey can be successfully taken, the individual's mindset must begin its transformational journey where he/she can accept that business as usual is a myth and everyday changes are made that help each Christian accept the changes bombarding their life instead of resisting them. I am forced to ask the following question: Did Sarai realize that while on her collective and personal journey God was requiring her to change; to become the woman, He knew was inside of her waiting to come out? The word of God says, "*I have hidden thy word in my heart…*" (Psalm 119:11) What concerns me is what else has been hidden in there encased in stone and hindering the Christian from fully maximizing the intent and message of Psalm 119:11. It is from Psalms 119:11 that the true meaning and realization of Proverbs 4:23, "*Keep your heart with all vigilance, for from it flows the springs of life…*" can be realized. The challenges Sarah faced may seem trivial to some but to her they were monumental. It had everything to do with perspective and reality. At no time did faith play into the choices Sarah made. Her choices were based solely upon her emotional state and her five (5) senses. According to the Tufts article, *"Emotion and Our Senses"* dated 10/9/2014 by Rebekah Rago, *"Beyond our perception, our senses play an integral role in our emotional processing, learning and interpretation… our emotions and senses are tightly intertwined… and can provide us with information on how to feel."* As I continued to research the issue, I learned that *"emotions can affect not just the nature of the decision, but the speed at which you make it."* The article also says, *"emotions are created when the brain interprets what's going on around us through our memories, thoughts and beliefs. This triggers how we feel and behave. All our decisions are influenced by this process in some way."*

One of the biggest challenges any Christian faces and struggles with from time to time is whether or not to trust God fully and wholly. Sarai's journey through barrenness to fulfillment is a prime example of this very thing. When she did not see a way for God's promise to be fulfilled, she resorted and reverted to the customs and ideologies that she was supposed to have left behind when she began this journey. It is almost as if she failed to see and accept the NEW THING (Isaiah 43:19) that God was desiring to perform in and through her. Her actions opened a door that couldn't be closed and set God's promise in a different direction than was originally intended. However, God knew Sarai's heart and provided a way of escape (1 Corinthians

10:13) for her even when her choices caused unexpected and tenuous consequences that infected, affected and birthed a nation.

As I began looking at Genesis 16 again, I realized that there was a section heading that spoke to the motivation behind Sarai's actions. The section heading was listed as "unbelief and impatient." Unbelief is defined as an absence of faith; a lack of religious belief; and impatience is defined as the quality of not wanting to put up with or wait for something or someone; lack of patience; restless. These two (2) words forced me to take another look at Sarai and realize that Sarai acted in a manner that went against the promise at face value and spoke to exactly where she was with the whole thing: acting with the absence of faith and the lack of patience because she could only see what she could see: barrenness. It goes back to something God showed me recently; people can only see what they can see when they see it. Their focus is only on what is directly affecting and infecting their world in that moment. That is what it was with Sarai, she depended upon the customs and ideologies of her past to move their life from expectation to realization. She failed to understand the importance of waiting on God to take the necessary actions to move the promise from spoken words to fulfillment through the manifestation of the promised thing. I submit to you it was a colossal failure. Instead of her benefiting from the actions she performed, she became despised by the gift presented and began to rethink her previous plan. The child Hagar carried became a bone of contention for Sarai causing her to face what was really bothering her; she was jealous of Hagar because she gave to Abram what she, herself, could not give to him. Which in turn forced her to regret her action and hate the child born from Abram and Hagar's union. However, once Sarai's plan was put into motion there was no taking it back. It had to play out as God intended and not how Sarai expected. When we are operating under the umbrella of God's promises, we have to take them at face value. Just like in the Bible, we are told we are not to add anything to or take anything away from God's word (Deuteronomy 4:2, Revelation 22:18-19); or away from God's promises. We are to believe God and have faith that in His timing He will manifest His promises in our reality.

EMOTIONAL INTELLIGENCE: Throughout Sarah's story, we see her making rash and emotional decisions that quite literally places the nation of Israel at odds with its brother nation, the Ishmaelites (Psalms 83:1-8) "…*For lo, thine enemies make a tumult; and they that hate thee… have said, Come, and let us cut them off from being a nation; that the name of Israel may be no more in remembrance… they are confederate against thee; the tabernacles of Edom, and Ishmaelites; of Moab, and the Hagarenes…*" (*How our emotions effect decision making,* www.BachRemedies.com blog) Throughout history we find women who have acted out based upon their emotional state in the same way that the Matriarchs of Genesis have. While focusing in on Sarah as it relates to her relationship with Hagar, it shows Sarah's lack of Emotional Intelligence (EI).

It is important to consider the time period in which Hagar enters into Sarah's life and how the introduction itself defines their relationship going forward personally and as a nation.

In Genesis 12, we find God instructing Abram to leave his homeland and father's house to travel to the land of Canaan. A famine comes into the land where Abram and his companions are residing forcing Abram and his family to sojourn to Egypt. As they were entering Egypt, Abram tells Sarai to only reveal that she is his sister and not that she is also his wife for fear that they'd kill him and take her to be a part of Pharaoh's harem because of her beauty. During her stay in Pharaoh's palace during her preparation to become his wife; two (2) things happen: (1) the Lord plagued Pharaoh and his house with great plagues, and (2) Sarai is gifted with a maidservant, Hagar, to assist with her marriage preparations as her personal maid. (Genesis 12:14-20)

Even though God reveals Abram's deception to Pharaoh, there are no consequences placed upon Abram and Sarai other than them being expelled from Egypt with all that he had and had acquired from the Egyptians when Sarai was taken to become one (1) of Pharaoh's wives and a part of his harem (Genesis 12:18-20; 15:16). This is the beginning, a relationship built upon a deception and continued servitude for Hagar. While considering Sarai's actions we must also look at Hagar's emotional state. Hagar was placed under Sarai's leadership for one (1) reason and when that reason ceased to exist Hagar remained in servitude while being forced to leave her homeland and all she knew behind her. Hagar was forced to learn Abram and Sarai's customs while being introduced to a God she had never heard about before. That alone is enough to send Hagar into a spiraling depression. However, that wasn't Hagar's reality. She had a job to do forcing her to push all of that down into a corner of her heart and close the door on it. Hagar had to learn how to survive amongst these strangers who live by strange cultures and beliefs in order to serve her mistress as she had been trained to do.

What we need to keep in mind is that both Hagar and Sarai were in very vulnerable states. They were both forced into situations that they were mentally, emotionally and Spiritually unprepared to handle. Although each was experiencing the newfound relationship differently, we can agree that they were experiencing "...*the roots of anger, hatred and disgust...*" (*Just emotions: Reading the Sarah and Hagar narrative (Genesis 16, 21) through the lens of human dignity*, http://www.scielo.org.za, by Juliana Claassens, January 2013) so deep that they experienced a sense of hopelessness that caused them to respond in a negative manner. They each were feeling like they had no control over the situation, not even their bodies. Hagar found herself pregnant and experiencing all that entailed, while Sarah began experiencing a jealousy and ineptness that left her hating the very thing she had intended to cherish. It is the same for each Christian, especially when we attempt to help God out and the consequences are more than we expected, can handle and/or bargained for. They not only found themselves fighting for control but also for some type of dignity that would allow them to hold their heads up and keep moving forward even though the situation took them places they never expected to go while experiencing feelings they are ill equipped to handle. All of this leads me to ask, how is barrenness represented in Sarah's life? Sarai's physical condition is a bone of contention in her life, and in her role within the family. Think about it for a minute, the greatest accomplishment and purpose for any woman born in this day and time is to bare children, specifically a male child. Knowing her body in essence has turned against her must have caused Sarai a great deal of pain. Pain that was magnified in intensity every time she had her monthly flow indicating no pregnancy. In desperation, Sarai begins to make decisions and choices while emotionally unstable and/or emotionally charged. This speaks to Sarai's lack of emotional intelligence in her life, in her marriage and as Hagar's mistress.

EMOTIONAL INTELLIGENCE (EI): is the ability to understand and manage your own emotions, and those of the people around you; and know what you are feeling, what your emotions mean, and how your emotion can/will affect others. The five (5) characteristics of emotional intelligence are self-awareness; self-regulation; motivation; empathy and social skills:

According to the *"Just Emotions,"* article, *Sarai's actions, choices and/or behaviors speak to the internal battle between Sarai's emotions and the moral code/ethics that Sarai learned early in life.* The article says, *"In the story of Sarah and Hagar, it is clear that Sarah, due to her inability to bear children, needs Hagar and is drawn to her* (as a surrogate). *But we also see the ambivalence at the heart of this desire when Sarai turns on Hagar in an expression of profound disgust."* A *"…disgust that causes one to create distance between the self and the object or subject he or she finds disgusting."* This is clearly seen in Genesis 16 where Sarai plans to help God fulfill His word/promise to Abram when she offers her handmaid to Abram as a concubine and in her stead to conceive, carry and birth the promised seed. As we see in the scriptures, Sarai's lack of EI and the internal war between her emotions and her moral compass results in an unexpected change in Hagar and Sarai's relationship. According to Genesis 16:4-6 *"…when she saw that she (Hagar) had conceived; her mistress (Sarai) was despised in her (Hagar) eyes… my wrong be upon thee: I have given my maid into thy bosom… I was despised in her (Hagar) eyes."* In response to Sarai's emotional plea to Abram, he tells Sarai *"…do to her as it pleaseth thee."* When Sarai dealt harshly with her (Hagar), she fled from her (Sarai's) face. Which clearly shows that … *the immediate effect of disgust …causes the subject* (Sarai) *to create distance between the self and the object* (Hagar) *…she finds disgusting.* Thereby creating necessary boundaries that speak to the roles each woman will play going forward. In all of this, one (1) thing that God showed me is that when we act outside of His will and interject our will into the equation, the outcome brings forth consequences that cannot be fathomed or even considered as the storyline continues in the lives of Abram, Sarai and Hagar. As previously discussed, Hagar submits to her mistress, Sarai, and endures what that looks like for both women with Abram being a spectator to this newly defined relationship as he continues on his journey from promise to fulfillment. Throughout time we have heard how the object meant to be the solution for the desired outcome becomes the despised object because it unexpectedly showcases the weaknesses or inadequacies in such a way that it is more than can be received and/or handled by the individual at that moment in time.

PARENTHETICAL CITATION: With regard to the story of Sarah and Hagar one sees how the repeated reference to Hagar, the Egyptian, serves the function of sharply drawing the boundaries between Israel and one of her most significant neighbors. Tikva Frymer-Kensky (2002:232-233) has pointed out that this narrative of Sarah and Hagar ought to be read in the larger context of Israel's sojourn in Egypt where the roles of master or slave is dramatically reversed. *It thus seems that the micro-story of Sarah's personal crisis of not being able to bear a child and her treatment of her servant Hagar can be read on a macro-level of Israel contemplating their relationship with the Egyptians under whose hand they suffered serious affliction as narrated in the book of Exodus.* So, even though the Egyptian slave woman Hagar is the object of the scorn and contempt of her Israelite mistress, Sarah, a couple of chapters later in Exodus 1, it will be the Israelites who find themselves in bondage;

when the Egyptians are in a position of power and the Israelites are the slaves serving their harsh slave masters... It may well be that Israel's sojourn in Egypt is responsible for facilitating this contact zone between Israel and Egypt - a significant relationship that is equaled by Israel's tumultuous relationship with her neighboring nations in Canaan. *(Just emotions: Reading the Sarah and Hagar narrative (Genesis 16:21) through the lens of human dignity, http://www.scielo.org.za, by Juliana Claassens, January 2013)*

In EI there are five (5) characteristics that are found in an emotionally intelligent individual. As we take a look at each of these, consider where Sarai falls into each as Hagar's mistress and a leading lady in the *Desperate Housewives of Biblical Proportions: The Birth of a Nation*.

EMOTIONAL INTELLIGENCE (EI) CHARACTERISTICS:

1. **Self-awareness**: You always know how you feel and know when your emotions or your actions can affect the people around you. It speaks to your ability to have a clear picture of your strengths and weaknesses and behaving with humility.
2. **Self-regulation**: The ability to regulate yourself effectively while rarely verbally attacking others, making rushed or emotional decisions, stereotyping people or compromising your values. This character is all about having self-control and speaks to your commitment to personal accountability.

3. **Motivation**: A self-motivated person works consistently towards their goals and has extremely high standards for the quality of their work and their interactions with others. This person always tries to find at least one (1) good thing about the situation.
4. **Empathy**: Having empathy is critical to living a life with EI. A person with empathy has the ability to put themselves in someone else's situation. This person opens themselves up to help others develop and grow into well rounded and empathetic individuals.
5. **Social Skills**: This person is a great communicator and is good at managing change and resolving conflicts diplomatically. This person sets the example of having effective social skills by being its living example with their own behaviors.

Before God can take Sarah any further Spiritually while on her journey, she must learn the importance of becoming emotionally intelligent. As we have previously read, Sarah was emotionally immature in how she made major life choices and decisions based upon her current emotional state. This is apparent in her relationship with Hagar after conceiving Ishmael. Prior to Sarai offering Hagar to Abram, we surmise that Sarai trusted and respected Hagar as much as a mistress can trust a servant. However, when faced with seeing her experience with barrenness up close and personal it was more than Sarai could handle emotionally and mentally. The one (1) thing she desired and treasured; and the true reason for the offering became despised, even hated, in Sarai's eyes. Why? Because it was a constant reminder of Sarai's shame, embarrassment, inabilities, barrenness and/or failings. Sarai became unable to see past her emotions to accept and even visualize the promises God made to Abram and to her by default. As I have said before, Sarai could only see what she could see. And for 14 years she took her inadequacies, her hatred for her barrenness, her shame and her emotional instability out on Hagar, which speaks to Sarai's struggle with emotional intelligence.

In Sarai/Sarah's storyline as a matriarch in Genesis, we are unable to see where Sarai/Sarah is self-aware of how her actions negatively affected Hagar, Ishmael and even Abram/Abraham. In her discourse with Hagar in Genesis 16:4-6, we find Sarai/Sarah verbally attacking Hagar with such fierceness that Hagar flees from the pure hatred and disgust Sarai/Sarah now holds for Hagar and her unborn child. After the conception and birth of Ishmael it is as if Sarai resigns herself to the fact that she will not bare the promised seed even though she's assured the promise is to be fulfilled in her. She cannot see it, which speaks of her inability to accept it. Without realizing it, Sarah gives God the opening He needs to perform a miracle in and through Sarah as He performs the promises made to Abram/Abraham.

In everything that we have read and learned of Sarai/Sarah, we can clearly see that she lacked the skills needed to show Hagar, Ishmael and even Abram/Abraham empathy when she demands that Abraham cast Hagar and Ishmael from the housing and the protection of the camp to have their own wilderness experience that ultimately ends in God saving them alive. Without realizing it, Sarah began a tumultuous relationship between Isaac's descendants (Israelites) and Ishmael's descendants (Muslims) that has reverberated throughout time and is shown in the lives of the Muslims and Jews in modern day Israel. In everything we have learned about Sarai/Sarah, one (1) thing has become abundantly clear that Sarah never truly learned how to play nice with others. She was fiercely loyal to those she loved, to distraction. However, she had no tolerance for those who she perceived desired to interfere with those relationships in any way. If nothing else, we can learn how destructive Sarah's attributes and behaviors can be in the life of any Christian. Although God wants us to build an intimate and personal relationship with Him, it cannot become a distraction. That relationship is to inspire, encourage, empower and be the living example to every Christian on how to live out Matthew 28:16-20 in their daily walk, and various interactions with people of all walks of life, personalities and lifestyles.

MENOPAUSE. In Genesis 18:10, we find the Lord visiting with Abram and the visitation of God's three (3) emissaries when he says, "*I will certainly return unto thee according to the time of life; and Sarah thy wife shall have a son.*" The part of the scripture that we will first focus on is "*I will certainly return unto thee according to the time of life…*" This began to speak to me and show me that God, in all His wisdom, was making a promise of how he would perform the last part of the scripture "*…Sarah thy wife shall have a son.*" As you have read, Sarah is well past childbearing years. As a matter of fact, Sarah is in her late 80's when the conversation takes place. Meaning she has surpassed childbearing age, menopause and is well into old age. When Sarah overhears the conversation, she laughs. Why did she laugh? She laughed because of unbelief. She did not look at the promise through eyes of faith. She looked at the promise through eyes of reality because her current situation required her to believe that this promise would never become a reality. Why? Because she was only capable of believing what she could see and not seeing what she believed. Her vision was distorted to the point that she was focused on her current physical and physiological condition. Why is this answer significant? Because it would take a miracle for Sarah to conceive and have a son. A miracle that is promised to happen in Genesis 18:10 "*I will certainly return unto thee according to the time of life…*" In today's reality what will that need to look like? Sarah's body would have to be returned to a state of preparation for conception. Let's look at the significance of the second stage of Sarai's life, menopause.

MENOPAUSE: the transitional period in a woman's life when her ovaries start producing less of the sex hormones estrogen and progesterone and is declared when a woman ceases to have a menstrual period for 12 consecutive months, marking the end of her reproductive years.

Typically, a woman experiences menopause between the ages 45 and 50. Meno is borrowed from the Greek, where it means "month," and Pause (pausis) is a *"cessation, a pause"* from Pauen *"to cause to cease."*

The entire process to reverse a woman's ability to conceive happens during menopause and what God was proclaiming would require the reverse to be reversed and Sarah's barren state to be addressed. The level of preparation Sarah's body needed to go through was immense from a medical and physiological standpoint. In this very intimate conversation, God reiterates the time in which conception will occur after He promises to "…*return unto thee according to the time of life…*" I am going to allow that to sit right there for a minute. Just take a minute and marinate on the message God is giving us. God is calling "…*those things which be not as though they were…*" (Romans 4:17) into and over Sarah's current medical and physiological condition. Something that seems medically and physiologically impossible in our reality, however, I challenge you to consider Genesis 18:14 *"Is anything too hard for the Lord…"*

As previously stated, God would have to reverse the reversed (normal menopausal state) and address her barrenness. Upon further review, I realized that God had to miraculously prepare Sarah's body for conception meaning He would have to heal any and all physiological, medical, mental and emotional issues to prepare her and her body for conception. While preparing her womb to receive and carry the promised seed, God had to take Sarah's reproductive organs back to its youthful state prior to menopause for conception and the impending pregnancy. Just think, try to imagine the unimaginable while stretching your heart and mind to experience the miraculous work of God is next to impossible.

In most cases a woman who is experiencing barrenness is considered to be sterile. Sterility is the result of the woman experiencing hormonal problems with one (1) of the issues being a failure to produce mature eggs (anovulation). The medical condition, Anovulation, is when the ovaries are not producing normal follicles in which eggs, necessary for reproduction, can mature leaving the woman unable to conceive and believed to be sterile. (*Infertility Treatment: An Overview – What causes female infertility?*) It is this process that God must heal as He speaks a word of healing into and over Sarai/Sarah's body, and mental and emotional states which is also seen in Matthew 8:8-13, when Jesus speaks a word of healing and the individual is made whole. "*The centurion answered and said, Lord, I am not worthy that thou shouldest come under my roof; but speak the word only, and my servant shall be healed… And Jesus said unto the centurion, go thy way; and as thou hast believed, so be it done unto thee. And his servant was healed in the selfsame hour.*"

Let's backtrack for a moment, remember having a child is all that Sarah wanted, and not just any child but a son. However, Sarah never prepared herself to be an active participant of nor to complete her role in the promise. Sarah realized early on that the only benefit the promise has for her is in its fulfillment. Other than that Sarah does not show that she is committed to or even believes the promise will happen. It's because of this that Sarah laughs. She laughs because it all sounds good, but it isn't a reality as far as she is concerned. In today's society, a woman who is struggling with infertility will do whatever the doctor instructs to help her body prepare to conceive and carry a child. After hearing the promise made to Abram on several different occasions, Sarah did not work to transform her mind or her body in preparation of receiving the promise. Her inaction gave room for God to perform a miracle in and through her as He fulfilled His promise to Abram. A promise that literally resulted in the birth of a nation.

As we continue to take this journey into understanding Sarah, her actions and/or motivations, we have to take into consideration that God used in Sarah what she thought was "...*wasted or empty*..." (Steven Furick, 5/17/2020, "*Flex Space*" sermon) to fulfill a promise and His will. Sarah failed to see and visualize what God spoke to Abraham and is the reason why Sarah, offered Hagar to Abram, became jealous of Hagar and Ishmael and laughed. The fulfillment of the promise seemed so far from reality for Sarah especially since there was literally 39 years from promise to performance in Sarah and Abraham's life. Each of us act without faith from time to time because we are unable to see and/or visualize what God has spoken into our heart and Spirit. If you seriously look at Sarah, some of us will be looking at a mirror image of our self. Looking at where we are with a renewed anticipation of where God is taking us. Of how His promises will manifest themselves into our reality when and if we submit to His will. Just like with Sarah, each of our *"…emotions can affect not just the nature of our decisions but the speed at which you make it… emotions are created when the brain interprets what's going on around us through our memories, thoughts and beliefs. This triggers how we feel and behave. All our decisions are influenced by this process in the same way."* (How do our emotions effect decision making," www.BachRemedies.com blog)

Keeping in mind the promises God made to Abraham in Genesis 12:1-3, we see it play out in their interactions with both King Abimelech and the Pharaoh. In Genesis 12:17, we find Pharaoh's house being struck with a great plague the entire time that Pharaoh had Sarai causing Pharaoh to return Sarai to Abram untouched. Upon Sarai's return, the plague was lifted, and Sarai and Abram continued on their journey richer than before. This is the first instance of Pharaoh experiencing the power and strength of the God of the Israelites and is a catalyst in the later interactions between the Egyptians and Israelites.

In Genesis 20:2, King Abimelech took Sarah unto himself and while Sarah was a part of King Abimelech's household, God closed up all the wombs of his household until Sarah was returned to Abram untouched. Here we see an already rich Abram given sheep, oxen, servants and land when Sarah is restored to Abram and they are sent on their way. When they leave, Abraham prays, and God restored King Abimelech's household. Even as children of God today, we must act in integrity and in ways that'll bring God glory. Because of the promises God made Abram in Genesis chapter 12, He is bound to ensure Abram's safety, to provide for him and his household and to take him from promise to performance to ensure His will is accomplished concerning Abraham and Sarah.

When I was married, I prayed continuously for my husband. My prayers were specific and included him coming to know Jesus as his savior and develop a personal and intimate relationship with Him. I remember discussing this with my mother-in-love, and she said she was praying as well. During that conversation, we both revealed that God had told us both that because of His relationship with each of us, He is duty bound to answer our individual and collective prayers and that by doing so it would not speak to His will for Steve, my ex-husband. That if we trusted Him, to quit praying our specific prayers and just pray for God's will to be done in his life. Just as His will had to supersede our specific prayers in Steven's life; the performance of God's promises had to play out in Abraham's and Sarah's lives, as well. No matter the situation, God's will for His people will always play out in their reality depending upon their relationship with Him. Sometimes it is necessary for God to develop us Spiritually and to heal and deliver us from our relationship with BARRENNESS, in the same way He did with both Hagar and Sarah. With this knowledge every child of God can live out Colossians 4:12b: "*…stand perfect and fully assured in all the will of God.*"

SPIRITUAL MENOPAUSE: When a woman experiences a period of grief that is seemingly never-ending. A grief that is a facet of a powerful emotional death/rebirth process because she knows, deep within her heart, that there is much more to being a woman beyond the superficiality of only birthing children. She grieves because this inexplicable loss seems almost unbearable, not yet knowing that her forthcoming blessings will be richly bountiful, but first she must experience emptiness, and because she has not been seen, understood and/or loved; the process takes her to depths that she has never experienced before while leaving her insecure, uncertain and depressed. However, when the beautiful cup, the holy chalice of her womb has been emptied of its grief, she begins to prepare for a life of deepening wisdom and grace-filled peace that begins to fill her cup with the bountiful richness of new blessings. During her menopausal journey, the repressed pain that she has worn like a piece of clothing is released and the wise and loving consciousness within her seeks release as she mourns the loss of all that she's held dear, seen as her personal definers and as her reason for living can never be again.

Although Sarah was barren her true relationship with barrenness came from her emotional immaturity and her inability to visualize/believe in the promises God made with

Abraham. Even though she was not the holder of the promise, she was responsible for conceiving and birthing the promise. Like many Christians today, Sarah could only see what she could see. God was challenging her to change and to see things with her Spiritual eyes, however, she didn't get or understand what God was trying to do in and with her life. Sarah was being stretched by God to believe and accept a promise that in reality didn't seem possible. Quite simply it was outside of her normal modus operandi and outside of her scope of understanding. God required something of her that He knew she was not capable of doing or ever considered on her own.

We find Sarah having her own experience with Spiritual Menopause that was effectively dealt with when God stepped in and began His perfect work in her life. He removed the negative connotation that had been stamped upon Sarah's life when He manifested His promise to *"…return unto thee according to the time of life…"* In that one (1) miraculous act, God shows us that although women were given the ability to birth children, we are so much more than that one (1) ability. That our life has meaning even after that ability is removed and we are able to step into our own as powerful and wise women of substance and of God.

LET'S TALK ABOUT IT. While thinking about Sarai/Sarah's and Abram/Abraham's journey, we can surmise that they both experienced four (4) things. The challenge here is to consider that although they were on the same journey, how they both experienced their collective journey differently. Why? Because of their relationship with God. In Abram/Abraham we find: 1) He was open to hear from God (Genesis 12:1); 2) Followed God's instructions (even when the ending was not made clear to him) (Genesis 12:4); 3) Trusted God at His word (Genesis 15:4-5; Hebrews 11:10,12); and 4) Committed to the Process (accepted that from promise to performance took years; it was not immediate) (Genesis 21:1-5). Whereas, in Sarai/Sarah we find: 1) Difficulty in leaving behind those things that aren't necessary on her journey with God (Genesis 16:1-2); 2) Discovering her TRUE identity in God (allowing God to heal her and deal with her Spiritual Menopause) (Genesis 21:6-7; Hebrews 11:11); 3) God's Timing isn't Sarai/Sarah's timing (just because it doesn't happen when she desires it to happen, doesn't mean it won't happen) (Genesis 18:12-13; 21:1-3) and 4) Understand that she controls her emotional wellbeing (not allow her emotions to control her) (Genesis 16:4; 21:9-10).

Think about your own Christian journey, in what ways are you holding on to aspects of the before Christ (BC) you, that doesn't really have a place in the now Christ (NC) you? What are some honest examples of how you have one (1) foot in the BC you and one foot in the NC you? How is this position speaking to the decisions, choices and actions you take daily in your walk with Christ? Read Revelation 3:16, what message is God giving you regarding this practice?

In what ways are you experiencing Spiritual menopause during your walk with Christ? How has the placement of your feet (as it relates to the previous questions) play into your ability to visualize the promises God has made to you, your family, etc.

BIBLE GUIDE QUESTIONS:

1. Who is Sarai/Sarah?

2. What challenges do Sarai/Sarah face?

3. In what way(s) does Sarai/Sarah attempt to help God out? What is it really representative of?

4. What is Sarai/Sarah's role in the Promise made to Abraham?

_____

_____

_____

_____

_____

5. What are your take-a-ways from Sarai/Sarah's character analysis?

_____

_____

_____

_____

_____

THE DESTRUCTIVENESS OF FAVORITISM

(Genesis 24:60 – 67; 25:19 – 28:9)

SCRIPTURE LESSON: GENESIS 24:60-67: *⁶⁰And they blessed Rebekah, and said unto her, Thou art our sister, be thou the mother of*

thousands of millions, and let thy seed possess the gate of those which hate them. ⁶¹ And Rebekah arose, and her damsels, and they rode upon the camels, and followed the man: and the servant took Rebekah and went his way. ⁶² And Isaac came from the way of the well Lahairoi; for he dwelt in the south country. ⁶³ And Isaac went out to meditate in the field at the eventide: and he lifted up his eyes, and saw, and, behold, the camels were coming. ⁶⁴ And Rebekah lifted up her eyes, and when she saw Isaac, she lighted off the camel. ⁶⁵ For she had said unto the servant, What man is this that walketh in the field to meet us? And the servant had said, It is my master: therefore she took a vail, and covered herself. ⁶⁶ And the servant told Isaac all things that he had done. ⁶⁷ And Isaac brought her into his mother Sarah's tent, and took Rebekah, and she became his wife; and he loved her: and Isaac was comforted after his mother's death.

GENESIS 25: 19 – 28:9: ¹⁹ And these are the generations of Isaac, Abraham's son: Abraham begat Isaac: ²⁰ And Isaac was forty years old when he took Rebekah to wife, the daughter of Bethuel the Syrian of Padanaram, the sister to Laban the Syrian. ²¹ And Isaac intreated the LORD for his wife, because she was barren: and the LORD was intreated of him, and Rebekah his wife conceived. ²² And the children struggled together within her; and she said, If it be so, why am I thus? And she went to enquire of the LORD. ²³ And the LORD said unto her, Two nations are in thy womb, and two manner of people shall be separated from thy bowels; and the one people shall be stronger than the other people; and the elder shall serve the younger. ²⁴ And when her days to be delivered were fulfilled, behold, there were twins in her womb. ²⁵ And the first came out red, all over like an hairy garment; and they called his name Esau. ²⁶ And after that came his brother out, and his hand took hold on Esau's heel; and his name was called Jacob: and Isaac was threescore years old when she bare them. ²⁷ And the boys grew: and Esau was a cunning hunter, a man of the field; and Jacob was a plain man, dwelling in tents. ²⁸ And Isaac loved Esau, because he did eat of his venison: but Rebekah loved Jacob. ²⁹ And Jacob sod pottage: and Esau came from the field, and he was faint: ³⁰ And Esau said to Jacob, Feed me, I pray thee, with that same red pottage; for I am faint: therefore was his name called Edom. ³¹ And Jacob said, Sell me this day thy birthright. ³² And Esau said, Behold, I am at the point to die: and what profit shall this birthright do to me? ³³ And Jacob said, Swear to me this day; and he sware unto him: and he sold his birthright unto Jacob. ³⁴ Then Jacob gave Esau bread and pottage of lentiles; and he did eat and drink, and rose up, and went his way: thus Esau despised his birthright.

GENESIS 26: *And there was a famine in the land, beside the first famine that was in the days of Abraham. And Isaac went unto Abimelech king of the Philistines unto Gerar. ² And the* LORD *appeared unto him, and said, Go not down into Egypt; dwell in the land which I shall tell thee of: ³ Sojourn in this land, and I will be with thee, and will bless thee; for unto thee, and unto thy seed, I will give all these countries, and I will perform the oath which I sware unto Abraham thy father; ⁴ And I will make thy seed to multiply as the stars of heaven, and will give unto thy seed all these countries; and in thy seed shall all the nations of the earth be blessed; ⁵ Because that Abraham obeyed my voice, and kept my charge, my commandments, my statutes, and my laws. ⁶ And Isaac dwelt in Gerar: ⁷ And the men of the place asked him of his wife; and he said, She is my sister: for he feared to say, She is my wife; lest, said he, the men of the place should* kill me for Rebekah; because she was fair to look upon. ⁸ And it came to pass, when he had been there a long time, that Abimelech king of the Philistines looked out at a window, and saw, and, behold, Isaac was sporting with Rebekah his wife. ⁹ And Abimelech called Isaac, and said, Behold, of a surety she is thy wife; and how saidst thou, She is my sister? And Isaac said unto him, Because I said, Lest I die for her. ¹⁰ And Abimelech said, What is this thou hast done unto us? one of the people might lightly have lien with thy wife, and thou shouldest have brought guiltiness upon us. ¹¹ And Abimelech charged all his people, saying, He that toucheth this man or his wife shall surely be put to death. ¹² Then Isaac sowed in that land, and received in the same year an hundredfold: and the LORD blessed him. ¹³ And the man waxed great, and went forward, and grew until he became very great: ¹⁴ For he had possession of flocks, and possession of herds, and great store of servants: and the Philistines envied him. ¹⁵ For all the wells which his father's servants had digged in the days of Abraham his father, the Philistines had stopped them, and filled them with earth. ¹⁶ And Abimelech said unto Isaac, Go from us; for thou art much mightier than we. ¹⁷ And Isaac departed thence, and pitched his tent in the valley of Gerar, and dwelt there. ¹⁸ And Isaac digged again the wells of water, which they had digged in the days of Abraham his father; for the Philistines had stopped them after the death of Abraham: and he called their names after the names by which his father had called them. ¹⁹ And Isaac's servants digged in the valley, and found there a well of springing water. ²⁰ And the herdmen of Gerar did strive with Isaac's herdmen, saying, The water is ours: and he called the name of the well Esek; because they strove with him. ²¹ And they digged another well, and strove for that also: and he called the name of it Sitnah. ²² And he removed from thence, and digged another well; and for that they strove *not: and he called the name of it Rehoboth; and he said, For now the LORD hath made room for us, and we shall be fruitful in the land. ²³ And he went up from thence to Beersheba. ²⁴ And the LORD appeared unto him the same night, and said, I am the God of Abraham thy father: fear not, for I am with thee, and will bless thee, and multiply thy seed for my servant Abraham's sake. ²⁵ And he builded an altar there, and called upon the name of the LORD, and pitched his tent there: and there Isaac's servants digged a well. ²⁶ Then Abimelech went to him from Gerar, and Ahuzzath one of his friends, and Phichol the chief captain of his army. ²⁷ And Isaac said unto them, Wherefore come ye to me, seeing ye hate me, and have sent me away from you? ²⁸ And they said, We saw certainly that the LORD was with thee: and we said, Let there be now an oath betwixt us, even betwixt us and thee, and let us make a covenant with thee; ²⁹ That thou wilt do us no hurt, as we have not touched thee, and as we have done unto thee nothing but good, and have sent thee away in peace: thou art now the blessed of the LORD. ³⁰ And he made them a feast, and they did eat and drink. ³¹ And they rose up betimes in the morning, and sware one to another: and Isaac sent them away, and they departed from him in peace.*

³² And it came to pass the same day, that Isaac's servants came, and told him concerning the well which they had digged, and said unto him, We have found water. ³³ And he called it Shebah: therefore the name of the city is Beersheba unto this day. ³⁴ And Esau was forty years old when he took to wife Judith the daughter of Beeri the Hittite, and Bashemath the daughter of Elon the Hittite: ³⁵ Which were a grief of mind unto Isaac and to Rebekah.

GENESIS 27: *And it came to pass, that when Isaac was old, and his eyes were dim, so that he could not see, he called Esau his eldest son, and said unto him, My son: and he said unto him, Behold, here am I. ² And he said, Behold now, I am old, I know not the day of my death: ³ Now therefore take, I pray thee, thy weapons, thy quiver and thy bow, and go out to the field, and take me some venison; ⁴ And make me savoury meat, such as I love, and bring it to me, that I may eat; that my soul may bless thee before I die. ⁵ And Rebekah heard when Isaac spake to Esau his son. And Esau went to the field to hunt for venison, and to bring it. ⁶ And Rebekah spake unto Jacob her son, saying, Behold, I heard thy father speak unto Esau thy brother, saying, ⁷ Bring me venison, and make me savoury meat, that I may eat, and bless thee before the LORD before my death. ⁸ Now therefore, my son, obey my voice according to that which I command thee. ⁹ Go now to the flock, and fetch me from thence two good kids of the goats; and I will make them savoury meat for thy father, such as he loveth: ¹⁰ And thou shalt bring it to thy father, that he may eat, and that he may bless thee before his death. ¹¹ And Jacob said to Rebekah his mother, Behold, Esau my brother is a hairy man, and I am a smooth man: ¹² My father peradventure will feel me, and I shall seem to him as a deceiver; and I shall bring a curse upon me, and not a blessing. ¹³ And his mother said unto him, Upon me be thy curse, my son: only obey my voice, and go fetch me them. ¹⁴ And he went, and fetched, and brought them to his mother: and his mother made savoury meat, such as his father loved. ¹⁵ And Rebekah took goodly raiment of her eldest son Esau, which were with her in the house, and put them upon Jacob her younger son: ¹⁶ And she put the skins of the kids of the goats upon his hands, and upon the smooth of his neck: ¹⁷ And she gave the savoury meat and the bread, which she had prepared, into the hand of her son Jacob. ¹⁸ And he came* unto his father, and said, My father: and he said, Here am I; who art thou, my son? ¹⁹ And Jacob said unto his father, I am Esau thy first born; I have done according as thou badest me: arise, I pray thee, sit and eat of my venison, that thy soul may bless me. ²⁰ And Isaac said unto his son, How is it that thou hast found it so quickly, my son? And he said, Because the LORD thy God brought it to me. ²¹ And Isaac said unto Jacob, Come near, I pray thee, that I may feel thee, my son, whether thou be my very son Esau or not. ²² And Jacob went near unto Isaac his father; and he felt him, and said, The voice is Jacob's voice, but the hands are the hands of Esau. ²³ And he discerned him not, because his hands were hairy, as his brother Esau's hands: so he blessed him. ²⁴ And he said, Art thou my very son Esau? And he said, I am. ²⁵ And he said, Bring it near to me, and I will eat of my son's venison, that my soul may bless thee. And he brought it near to him, and he did eat: and he brought him wine and he drank. ²⁶ And his father Isaac said unto him, Come near now, and kiss me, my son. ²⁷ And he came near, and kissed him: and he smelled the smell of his raiment, and blessed him, and said, See, the smell of my son is as the smell of a field which the LORD hath blessed: ²⁸ Therefore God give thee of the dew of heaven, and the fatness of the earth, and plenty of corn and wine: ²⁹ Let people serve thee, and nations bow down to thee: be lord over thy brethren, and let thy mother's sons bow down to thee: cursed be every one that curseth thee, and blessed be he that blesseth thee. ³⁰ And it came to pass, as soon as Isaac had made an end of blessing Jacob, and Jacob was yet scarce gone out from the presence of Isaac his father, that Esau his brother came in from his hunting. ³¹ And he also had made savoury meat, and brought it unto his father, and said unto his father, Let my father arise, and eat of his son's venison, that thy soul may bless me. ³² And Isaac his father said unto him, Who art thou?

And he said, I am thy son, thy firstborn Esau. ³³ *And Isaac trembled very exceedingly, and said, Who? where is he that hath taken venison, and brought it me, and I have eaten of all before thou camest, and have blessed him? yea, and he shall be blessed.* ³⁴ *And when Esau heard the words of his father, he cried with a great and exceeding bitter cry, and said unto his father, Bless me, even me also, O my father.* ³⁵ *And he said, Thy brother came with subtilty, and hath taken away thy blessing.* ³⁶ *And he said, Is not he rightly named Jacob? for he hath supplanted me these two times: he took away my birthright; and, behold, now he hath taken away my blessing. And he said, Hast thou not reserved a blessing for me?* ³⁷ *And Isaac answered and said unto Esau, Behold, I have made him thy lord, and all his brethren have I given to him for servants; and with corn and wine have I sustained him: and what shall I do now unto thee, my son?* ³⁸ *And Esau said unto his father, Hast thou but one blessing, my father? bless me, even me also, O my father. And Esau lifted up his voice, and wept.* ³⁹ *And Isaac his father answered and said unto him, Behold, thy dwelling shall be the fatness of the earth, and of the dew of heaven from above;* ⁴⁰ *And by thy sword shalt thou live, and shalt serve thy brother; and it shall come to pass when thou shalt have the dominion, that thou shalt break his yoke from off thy neck.* ⁴¹ *And Esau hated Jacob because of the blessing wherewith his father blessed him: and Esau said in his heart, The days of mourning for my father are at hand; then will I slay my brother Jacob.* ⁴² *And these words of Esau her elder son were told to Rebekah: and she sent and called Jacob her younger son, and said unto him, Behold, thy brother Esau, as touching thee, doth comfort himself, purposing to kill thee.* ⁴³ *Now therefore, my son, obey my voice; arise, flee thou to Laban my brother to Haran;* ⁴⁴ *And tarry with him a few days, until thy brother's fury turn away;* ⁴⁵ *Until thy brother's anger turn away from thee, and he forget that which thou hast done to him: then I will send, and fetch thee from thence: why should I be deprived also of you both in one day? ⁴⁶ And Rebekah said to Isaac, I am weary of my life because of the daughters of Heth: if Jacob take a wife of the daughters of Heth, such as these which are of the daughters of the land, what good shall my life do me?*

GENESIS 28: *And Isaac called Jacob, and blessed him, and charged him, and said unto him, Thou shalt not take a wife of the daughters of Canaan. ² Arise, go to Padanaram, to the house of Bethuel thy mother's father; and take thee a wife from thence of the daughters of Laban thy mother's brother. ³ And God Almighty bless thee, and make thee fruitful, and multiply thee, that thou mayest be a multitude of people; ⁴ And give thee the blessing of Abraham, to thee, and to thy seed with thee; that thou mayest inherit the land wherein thou art a stranger, which God gave unto Abraham. ⁵ And Isaac sent away Jacob: and he went to Padanaram unto Laban, son of Bethuel the Syrian, the brother of Rebekah, Jacob's and Esau's mother. ⁶ When Esau saw that Isaac had blessed Jacob, and sent him away to Padanaram, to take him a wife from thence; and that as he blessed him he gave him a charge, saying, Thou shalt not take a wife of the daughters of Canaan; ⁷ And that Jacob obeyed his father and his mother, and was gone to Padanaram; ⁸ And Esau seeing that the daughters of Canaan pleased not Isaac his father; ⁹ Then went Esau unto Ishmael, and took unto the wives which he had Mahalath the daughter of Ishmael Abraham's son, the sister of Nebajoth, to be his wife.*

INTRODUCTION

In the lives of Isaac and Rebekah, we find a clear path that plays out in their lives and the lives of their sons: the destructiveness of favoritism. In Isaac's life we find it early on when he witnesses as a young child the disdain, even the hatred, Sarah has for Hagar and Ishmael. He experienced having a big brother early in life only for him to be excommunicated and himself being raised not only as the promised seed but the favored son. That one (1) experience had its own impression in and upon Isaac's life that is seen in the scriptural journey I took to get to know Isaac. Isaac, unlike myself, never questioned nor stretched the boundaries to question the validity of the rules and/or to challenge the authorities in his life. In the story of Isaac, as found in the Life Application Bible, we find Isaac inheriting everything that belonged to Abraham, and realizing that nothing tangible was left to his brother, Ishmael nor his other half siblings. Not only did he receive the tangible things, but he also received the promises God made to his father, Abraham, to make his seed a great nation, to be a blessing or a curse upon those who blessed or cursed him and the knowledge that he's the favored son even though he is not Abraham's eldest son. This is significant in Isaac's life because it speaks to the even greater disparity and treatment, we find in both the lives of Ishmael and Isaac. According to the Firstborn (Judaism) in Wikipedia, *"the firstborn or the firstborn son is an important concept in Judaism. The role of the firstborn son carries significance in the redemption of the first-born son, in the allocation of a double portion of the inheritance, and in the prophetic application of 'first born' to the nation of Israel."* This is further clarified in the Rabbinical Interpretation, *"...the firstborn of one's mother as referred to in Exodus 13:2 as the one (1) who 'opens the womb' of his mother. Therefore, the firstborn of the father exclusively, although considered as a firstborn regarding his father's inheritance, is NOT considered as a firstborn of the mother (which) is the requirement to be redeemed... the Shulchan Auch (Code of Jewish Law) rules that only a first born to the mother is required to be redeemed."*

Think back to when God gives Abram the promises in Genesis chapter 12, it was at that time that Abram was married to Sarai and by default the promise included Sarai as she would be the one (1) to receive the seed, conceive and birth the promise as instructed or spoken of by God. This goes back even further to the importance of Sarai/Sarah's story as the mother of Isaac and her being the primary caregiver of Isaac during his initial formative years. This is even more clearly seen during the feast/celebration when Isaac was weaned and Sarah witnessed Ishmael doing what older siblings have done throughout the history of man, he teased and poked fun at his younger sibling, Isaac. I can almost imagine how Ishmael's teasing and poking had a harder bite to it especially since Isaac was favored by the same woman, Sarah, who for years had mistreated himself and his mother, Hagar. This mindset is supported in what Sarah says to Abraham in Genesis 21:10 *"Cast out this bondwoman and her son; for the son of this bondwoman shall not be heir with my son, even Isaac."* All of this and so much more molded Isaac into the son, man, husband and father we have read about in Genesis/Bible.

According to my research, *"...the personalities of only children are… they have higher levels of ambition, independence, character, and intelligence. They are also better adjusted. Contrary to popular belief, they are not more narcissistic or selfish... only children report a more positive relationship with parents. This is true in childhood as well as in adulthood. They even have better relationships with their… (and) also receive individual attention from parents as an infant. (https://researchaddict.com/only-child-effects/; The only child: everything you need to know, answered by research,* December 9, 2018, by Christa Spraggins) Isaac fully trusted and respected his father, Abraham, from the time, love and respect he received continuously from both is mother and father and in how he mourned Sarah's death for over three (3) years. His relationship with both parents seemed to be solid and clearly visible in how Isaac never resisted Abraham as a child, even when he is prepared as a sacrifice nor as a man when he gladly accepted the wife Abraham's most trusted servant presented to him. The life that Isaac lived prior to marrying Rebekah sets the scene of how any children born to them would be treated and how the destructiveness of favoritism crept in and played out in their lives and the lives of the nation of Israel for centuries to come. In Numbers 14:18 it says, "*…punishing the children for the sins of the parents to the third and fourth generations…*" As we begin the character analysis of Rebekah, the third matriarch of Genesis, we can clearly see her relationship with barrenness physically and in her participation in the destructiveness of favoritism and how it causes dissention, dishonesty and the fulfillment of prophecy in both her and Isaac's lives and the lives of her sons.

Throughout Genesis we find the storyline of many exceptional women whose choices, decisions and actions have greatly impacted a nation of people and Rebekah's story isn't any different. In the 24th chapter of Genesis we find Rebekah making her grand entrance into Abraham and Isaac's lives. Abraham gives his most trusted and eldest servant the task of returning to his family in Nahor to find a wife for Isaac. God blessed his obedience, patience and commitment by bringing Rebekah to him, and in her willingness to marry a kinsman she had yet to meet. Her immediate acceptance and willingness to take this journey, to leave her family and to be part of the promise God made to Abraham was rewarded in her immediate attraction to Isaac and Isaac's acceptance of Rebekah as his wife. Genesis 24:66-67 says, "*And the servant* (Eliezer) *told Isaac all things he had done. Isaac brought her* (Rebekah) *into his mother, Sarah's, tent and took Rebekah, and she became his wife; and he loved her; and Isaac was comforted after his mother's death.*"

Rebekah's willingness to be of service made it extremely easy for her to submit to Isaac as his wife. In the same way as it was easy for Isaac to love Rebekah because of the love showered on him by his parents and the security, he found in it along with his position within the family. Both of their pasts brought them together as a loving couple who although forced together accepted each other openly and the roles they would play in the family dynamic as the patriarch and matriarch of the Israelite nation. Their union meant more than just the coming together of two (2) people. It also represented the procreation of a nation of people that our Lord and Savior, Jesus Christ, Himself would be born into. I often wonder if they would have made different (or better) life choices had they had that bit of information beforehand.

REBEKAH

Rebekah is a feminine given name originating from the Hebrew language and comes from the verb meaning "to tie firmly". However, the Jones' Dictionary of Old Testament Proper Names and the NOBS Study Bible Name List suggest the name means captivating beauty, or "to tie", "to bind". Rebekah is the daughter of Bethuel, the great-niece of Abraham, and the sister of Laban. Her name speaks of both the magnetism of Rebekah's beauty and attraction that is felt when Isaac gazes upon her and marries her when he is forty years old.

Keep in mind that Rebekah came on the scene for a specific reason: as a wife for Isaac. According to Genesis chapter 24, Abraham sought a wife for his son that was not of the region and people in which they lived, the Canaanites, but of his family in Aram-Naharaim. Rebekah's, the third matriarch of Genesis, entrance into the story speaks to God's faithfulness and to His provisionary care of those who are in relationship with Him. Because of His relationship with Abraham and Eliezer, God began answering their collective prayers as spoken of by Eliezer before Eliezer even finished speaking it. What is amazing to me is that we see God operating in this manner in Bible days and is even operating in this manner today.

After marrying Isaac, it was 20 years before Rebekah conceived and birthed her son of prophecy. Like her mother-in-law, Rebekah has both a physical and Spiritual relationship with barrenness. Earlier I mentioned that God allowed these women to experience barrenness to heighten the excitement when the blessed event actually happened. Although I agree with that estimation, I must also add that I believe God allowed this to take place to build a relationship with these women as well. This is seen in how Isaac entreated of the Lord regarding Rebekah's barrenness, God heard him and opened her womb. It is seen in Rebekah during her pregnancy when she entreats the Lord as to the reason why she was experiencing such a difficult pregnancy. As Rebekah learned of the customs, rituals and beliefs that Abraham passed down to Isaac, she becomes familiar with the security and provisions given by this all-powerful God. It is my belief that the customs and rituals God gave Abraham were necessary in the lives of the children born to his ancestral line. So much so that God required the Israelites to "*…teach then diligently to your children, and shall talk of them when you sit in your house, and when you walk by the way, and when you lie down and when you rise.*" (Deuteronomy 6:7; 32:46; Genesis 18:19; Psalm 78:3-8; Proverbs 4:20-23)

THE SPIRIT OF ENTITLEMENT: As I write this character analysis, I am struck by how the favoritism both Isaac and Rebekah showed their sons became the foundation of the generational curse(s) that the Israelites have suffered through for centuries. Although Jacob is the son of prophecy his actions and decisions have reverberated throughout time in the lives of Jews and Gentiles alike. In my own life, the favoritism I was shown by my Father hindered my ability to develop a personal relationship with God while he lived, but is the foundation on which my relationship with God is built on today. The relationship with my Dad gave me the ingredients I combined to develop a sense of entitlement in my own life. Opening the door for me to believe I can have whatever I want or covet and would use any means necessary to have it. In that regard, I can relate to Jacob, however, because I loved my Dad dearly, deception was never a route I took with him to get what I wanted. I must admit I cannot say that concerning anyone else. In Rebekah's story, we find two (2) types of entitlement and how they played out in both Esau and Jacob's life as a direct reflection of the destructiveness of favoritism that is prevalent throughout their story and their relationship with their parents: Isaac and Rebekah.

ENTITLEMENT: The fact of having a right to something; the belief that one is inherently deserving of privileges or special treatment.

As the eldest son, Esau, was in line to receive a double blessing: the blessing of being the first born and the blessing of the promise that God made to his grandfather, Abraham. Throughout his childhood and the lessons taught by his father, Isaac, I am sure he is instructed as to the responsibilities that he has as the firstborn son that would one (1) day be passed down to him. However, Esau did not treat the birthright or the blessing with the honor and respect that he should have. In Genesis 25:29-34, *Esau ate and drank, pleased his palate, satisfied his appetite, and then carelessly rose up and went his way, without any serious thought, or any regret, about the poor choice he had made. (Commentary on Genesis 25:29-34, https://www.christianity.com/bible/commentary.php?com=mhc&b =1&c=25, Matthew Henry Concise Commentary)* Thereby, despising his birth-right by his neglect and disrespect.

The demand that Jacob put upon Esau shows that Jacob coveted Esau's birthright. What we must also consider is that although the birthright is Esau's by birth, it was literally Jacob's by prophecy. Regardless of the aforementioned fact, Jacob was dead wrong in taking advantage of his brother's desire for fulfillment. More than anything else these two (2) men's actions speak to their true individual personalities: Jacob's sense of entitlement and Esau's desire to gratify his sensual appetites. I find the need to remind you that Jewish customs dictate that the inheritance of their father's worldly goods did not descend to Jacob, naturally. However, by prophecy the birthright/blessing that included the future possession of the land of Canaan by his children's children, and the covenant made with Abraham as the progenitor of a great nation never belonged to Esau, but to Jacob.

This story of entitlement is clearly identified in an excerpt from *A Tale of Entitlement, August 29, 2012,* by *Jill Bakken* https://journal.christianscience.com/shared/view/1t31vaminys, that says, "*Entitlement is a prevalent concept in our society today. In the media there is a lot of talk about entitlement ... founded on a material* basis...Take, for example, the Bible story of Esau and Jacob... These brothers were twins, but because Esau was the older, he was entitled to a much greater inheritance than Jacob. Through deceit, ...Jacob twice tricked Esau out of his rightful entitlement, so Esau lost his birthright and his blessing—an inheritance that was legally his. And once it was lost, no matter how unjustly, he could not get it back."

GENERATIONAL CURSE: According to "The Four Generation Curse, by Larry Wood, September 23, 2016," www.biblenews1.com/curse4g/curse4g1.htm, "...God will tolerate negative volition in three or four kings before... the Divine decision to destroy the nation [is made]... the basis for blessing or cursing of the nation is the Grace of God related to the spirituality of the people. The rise or fall of the nation is based on God's attitude toward the people... [and their] ...spiritual [condition]. In both the Northern and Southern Kingdoms, the nation was destroyed... [for the] four (4) generations of negative volition... were the reason for the fall of the nation..."

GENERATIONAL CURSE: An uncleansed iniquity that increases in strength from one generation to the next, affecting the members of that family and all who come into relationship with that family. *"The LORD is longsuffering, and of great mercy, forgiving iniquity and transgression, and by no means clearing the guilty, visiting the iniquity of the fathers upon the children unto the third and fourth generation."* (Numbers 14:18)

A MOTHER'S INTERFERENCE: When Rebekah sought God about the difficulty of her pregnancy, she was told *"Two* *nations are in your womb, and two peoples from within you will be separated; one people will be stronger than the other and the older will serve the younger…"* (Genesis 25:23) Some Bible scholars suggest that there was an issue of ineffective communication in Isaac and Rebekah's marriage and home, and when the twins were born, the issues in their marriage became magnified. Basically, setting up the scenario of the perfect storm in which both Esau and Jacob became unwilling participants and unforeseen casualties. Keep in mind that Isaac and Rebekah are childless before Isaac prays to God for Rebekah, her womb is opened, and she conceives two (2) sons. According to Genesis 25:27, Esau is described as a skillful hunter, a man of the field and Jacob as a peaceful man, living in tents. It is speculated that as the children grew, the issues within Isaac and Rebekah's marriage got worse with each parent gravitating towards a different son. Thereby, creating an even deeper divide within the family unit. *"Isaac saw in Esau the rugged outdoorsman that he himself never was, and he learned to enjoy Esau's sporting exploits vicariously as he savored his delicious venison stew. Rebekah, on the other hand, favored Jacob. He stayed close to home. He probably talked to her, listened to her, and helped her with her chores. And she found with him the companionship she never enjoyed with her husband."* The article goes on to say *"Psychologists… tell us that a dominant mother and a passive father have a tendency to produce problem children, and that favoritism in the family unit tends to cause serious personality defects in the children… and contribute to low self-esteem and ambivalent feelings that confuse him and burden him with guilt."* Resulting in the child grasping for what he wants from life by any means necessary regardless of who he/she leaves hurt in his/her wake.

That want/desire previously mentioned is Jacob's desire to have Esau's birthright. Something he coveted and that fact, I am sure was well known by his mother, Rebekah. Without even truly considering it, Rebekah's actions and her deception further alienated her eldest son who seemed to disappoint her over and over again. When Rebekah found out that Esau threatened to kill her beloved Jacob, her devious mind goes into overdrive and she devises a masterful plan to get Jacob out of their home and away from Esau. That is until he calmed down. She complains once again about the wives that Esau has taken from amongst the Canaanites and states she does not want that for Jacob. Isaac agrees to send Jacob to Rebekah's brother and their people to find Jacob a wife. Little did Rebekah know that the last time she saw Jacob as he took his journey to visit his uncle, Laban, would be the last time she'd ever see him. Twenty (20) years later Jacob returns to the land of his birth with the realization that his mother has already died and is resting in the familial burial plot. The general pattern of Isaac and Rebekah's lives and that of their family has been and is being repeated in their ancestral family's homes throughout time. Even today we find couples who use their relationship with their children as a substitute for a good relationship with their mate/significant other.

Isaac and Rebekah's inability to love each other unconditionally, openly communicate, dependence upon deception as a way of life and their unwillingness to genuinely accept each other not only affected their sons: Esau and Jacob, but their behaviors and actions, and the sense of entitlement that both sons experienced continues in the story of the Israelites and is a foundational reason the Israelites were sent into captivity by the same God who favors them above all other nations. They believed that regardless of what they did God would always forgive them and continue to abide with them. In Genesis 6:3 KJV God says, "*…my Spirit shall not always strive with man, for that he is also flesh: yet his days shall be an hundred and twenty years.*" In the *Monthly Record, www.ChristianStudyLibrary.org, 1991* article on Genesis 6:1-3 by W. Macleod says "*…the sin committed by the Sethites (Seth's bloodline) when they chose to marry women from the ungodly Cainites (Cain's bloodline)* [was held to both of their charges by God] *because of* [their] *physical attractiveness* [and] *lust, rather than who would be good and godly mothers to their children. Where the upbringing of the families in the ways of the Lord was not a priority causing good and evil to co-mingle. These marriages had the opposite effect than expected, the Cainites progressed in their sin, pride and violence, and the Sethites grew indifferent to their spiritual heritage. In the history of Israel at a later date the same kind of catastrophe occurred. Balaam was offered a reward to destroy Israel… He got beautiful women of Moab to seduce the Israelites into immorality and then into idolatry. The plan succeeded and God's chastisement came upon Israel…*"

God will only allow His people to go so far before He brings chastisement upon them. Another example is when the Israelites spoke against God in Numbers 21:4-9 and God sent fiery serpents among the people causing many Israelites to die in the way. The invasion continued until the Israelites admitted their sin and asked for prayer resulting in Moses praying on their behalf and God sending a cure. However, that didn't stop the Israelites from sinning or speaking against God during their 40 year journey through the wilderness to the promised land. The same is seen in the lives of Christians today who believe that because they have accepted Jesus Christ as their Lord and Savior all they have to do when they sin is ask for forgiveness. Just like the Israelites, their sense of entitlement leaves them ignorant to the fact that every action has a comparable reaction, and every decision/choice has a consequence associated with it. It is what is known as the law of sowing and reaping or what we call today, Karma.

LAW OF SOWING AND REAPING. According to *"The 4 Laws of Sowing & Reaping and How they affect Your Marriage, www.theusequation.com, February 6, 2019 by Bradley Bennett, …all actions have consequences whether positive or negative. Everyone is planting seeds through actions or decisions that one day grows into a harvest that they will reap."* If we want to be honest, any and everyone can attest to this very thing taking place in their life. In my own life, God has always sent correction when I've lost my way and allowed the world's influence to guide or direct my path more than that of the Holy Spirit; to redirect me back to focusing on my relationship with Him. This normally happens after I have gone after something I desire or want while allowing my own feelings of entitlement to rear its ugly head and influence me to act contrary to my faith instead of practicing the law of binding and loosing. I find myself in a situation where I have failed to bind those feelings up and cast them in the pits of hell in Jesus' name and loose the healing powers of God's love into and over my heart, mind, body and Spirit while allowing God to continue to complete His perfect will in my life emotionally, mentally, physically and Spiritually.

DISCORD IN THE FAMILY. The prophecy given to Rebekah by God speaks to the continuous struggle the brothers experienced in the womb and their ancestors have experienced throughout time. Originally, Jacob coveted and took Esau's birthright/blessing through deception causing him to flee his homeland. During the time he is gone, he becomes the progenitor of a nation that is birthed from his loins; while his brother, Esau, is doing the very same thing and securing land and riches that's meant to be the legacy left for his ancestors, the Edomites. That may have been the intent, however, when Israel returns with his family to his homeland, he begins his quest to obtain the promises given to his forefather, Abraham. According to *"Why Were the Ancient Israelites and Edomites Enemies, www.dailyhistory.org,"* "*The first historical point of conflict between the Hebrews and Edomites took place… around the year 1200 BC, when the Hebrews* (Israelites) *left Egypt in the Exodus. As the Hebrews wandered* *throughout the Sinai Desert on their way to what would become their home in Canaan, they had to pass through Edom. According to the book of Numbers (20:17-20), the Edomites denied the Hebrews passage through their land… The book of Deuteronomy (2:1-8), states that the Hebrews were in fact allowed to pass through Edom. …the Edomites who allowed them to pass were in the southern, wilderness region of Edom. The circuitous route coincides with most of the likely Exodus routes, which would have sent the Hebrews …turning north and skirting the western edge of Edom… It is known, though, that there was no theological or religious conflict between the two peoples. By the time the Edomites and Israelites transitioned into kingdom states, land became a commodity that was exploited and taken by force… which proved to be at the core of the Israelite-Edomite conflict… When Israel became a kingdom… David… conquered Edom and, after doing so, installed permanent garrisons to ensure the Edomites would be compliant…"* In the prophecy given to Rebekah, it does not state how the older will serve the younger, only that it will happen. One would expect that it would have happened during the brother's lifetime, however, that isn't the case. It seems to play out in the ancestral lines of both brothers and the animosity that seemed to transcend time. One can even surmise, as generational curses played out in the lives of Esau's and Jacob's children's children its foundation began with how Rebekah interpreted and the role she played in the prophecy God spoke into and over her life, "*…two nations are in thy womb, and two manner of people shall be separated from thy bowels; and the one people shall be stronger than the other people; and the elder shall serve the younger…*"

CONCLUSION: While watching a movie, God showed me how and why the hardest most difficult and even abusive childhood experiences are important and has purpose in the life of those experiencing it and in those who encounter the child during their various phases of development. This is also true of Rebekah. The role she played as a matriarch in Genesis and her personal and Spiritual relationship with barrenness was necessary. She became the director in how the lives Isaac, Esau and Jacob lived, and how it played right into the prophecy that God had given to Rebekah. It speaks of the continuance of the Abrahamic covenant from one (1) generation to the next. Think about it!!! Rebekah's interpretation of the prophecy God gave her perpetrates her taking an active role in ensuring that Jacob receives the double blessing reserved for the first-born son. Every decision she made, every move she took, every action and reaction was strategically made to ensure that she did everything in her power to see the son of prophecy, Jacob, step into his prophetic role as explained by God on that fateful day when Rebekah's pregnancy became more than she could handle. What Rebekah did fell right in line with the history of the family and people that she married into. If you trace the lineage from Abraham through Judah, you will find that none of the first-born sons received the birthright nor the blessing of the Abrahamic covenant. I guess one would have to ask themselves, who would expect it to happen with Esau when it did not happen with anyone who came before or after Jacob?

In the same way that God uses flawed individuals to do extraordinary things, He used Rebekah to conceive, birth, raise and favor a son who would be the progenitor of the Israelite nation. The 12 sons born to him and their actions, deceptions, acts of disrespect, jealousy and feelings of inadequacy would ensure the continuation of their bloodline. (Genesis 50:20 has a resounding message in every generation of the Israelites and more than applies to Rebekah's actions, choices, her relationship with barrenness and the favoritism she displays towards Jacob that literally sets the nation of Israel up to be taken care of during their rough seasons; where it says, *"But as for you, ye thought evil against me; but God meant it unto good, to bring to pass, as it is this day, to save much people alive."* Just think of the journey that Joseph took from the pit to the palace because of the jealousy of his brother that directly resulted from the destructiveness of favoritism taught to Israel by his mother, Rebekah, and shown towards Joseph to the dismay of his brothers (Genesis 41:1-57); and how God used Joseph to provide for his family during difficult times. But I digress, let me get back to my point!

While Rebekah was living the story, we have been analyzing and telling, she had no idea how the part she played in how the destructiveness of favoritism would develop a nation in whom God favors and calls His very own. From the lowliest of positions, greatness is birthed and is why we should not despise Rebekah or think less of her for the role she played as a matriarch of the nation of Israel, her introduction of the Spirit of entitlement that was birthed from the favoritism that both her and her husband, Isaac, are guilty of, the generational curse(s) that was developed and can still be identified in the lives of the Israelite nation today and her interference to ensure Jacob stepped into his prophetic role as the father of the 12 tribes of Israel. All of this was necessary as God created a nation of people to call His own and because of their neglect, apostasy, sin and rejection it opened the door for Gentiles to be grafted in and develop a relationship with God through the perfect work Jesus did at Calvary.

Each of us have an opportunity to learn from Rebekah and her relationship with barrenness. We have before us a unique opportunity here! We have a real-life example of the destructiveness of favoritism and how ***not*** to allow it to be the foundation on which our individual relationship with barrenness is built upon. However, if it is, we have an advocate with the Father, by way of Jesus Christ, who is willing and able to heal us from all iniquity by beginning a great work of healing and deliverance in our lives that will give us the tools, faith and courage we need to end our relationship with barrenness and break the generational curses our relationship with barrenness has created and/or has the potential to create.

LET'S TALK ABOUT IT: Growing up I was told and/or the statement was made that I am spoiled. I did not understand it nor realize what that truly meant in my life then, but I do now! I am a product of the favoritism my Dad showed me while growing up and that at some point I began to take advantage of the privileges and the opportunities it afforded me. What I did not understand is how that innocently and lovingly given favoritism would turn into me having a relationship with barrenness where the spirit of entitlement would literally take me on a journey, I never expected nor intended to take. In the same way that my father never expected his actions to be played out in a negative way, I am sure Rebekah did not foresee how her favoritism would impact the two (2) nations of people birthed from her loins: the Edomites and the Israelites.

Take a minute and consider your upbringing and how you are raising or have raised your children, can you identify any of the same characteristics that Rebekah exhibited? Read Proverbs 22:6 and consider how you have or have not lived this scripture.

Bible Guide Questions:

1. Who is Rebekah and in what way is her story significant to you?

   _____

   _____

   _____

   _____

   _____

2. How did Rebekah's willingness to be of service pay off for her?

   _____

   _____

   _____

   _____

   _____

3. How did the Spirit of Entitlement become a generational curse for the nation of Israel?

   _____

   _____

   _____

4. How did Rebekah's interpretation of the prophecy God gave her, play out in the lives of the Israelite nation? Explain your answer while utilizing one (1) of the examples provided.

COMPARISON KILLS
THE DESPERATE HOUSEWIVES OF ISRAEL

SCRIPTURE LESSON: Genesis 29:13-35 – 30:25; Genesis 35:16-20

Genesis 29:13 – 35: *¹³And it came to pass, when Laban heard the tidings of Jacob his sister's son, that he ran to meet him, and embraced him, and kissed him, and brought him to his house. And he told Laban all these things. ¹⁴And Laban said to him, Surely thou art my bone and my flesh. And he abode with him the space of a month. ¹⁵And Laban said unto Jacob, Because thou art my brother, shouldest thou therefore serve me for nought? tell me, what shall thy wages be? ¹⁶And Laban had two daughters: the name of the elder was Leah, and the name of the younger was Rachel. ¹⁷Leah was tender eyed; but Rachel was beautiful and well favoured. ¹⁸And Jacob loved Rachel; and said, I will serve thee seven years for Rachel thy younger daughter. ¹⁹And Laban said, It is better that I give her to thee, than that I should give her to another man: abide with me. ²⁰And Jacob served seven years for Rachel; and they seemed unto him but a few days, for the love he had to her. ²¹And Jacob said unto Laban, Give me my wife, for my days are fulfilled, that I may go in unto her. ²²And Laban gathered together all the men of the place, and made a feast. ²³And it came to pass in the evening, that he took Leah his daughter, and brought her to him; and he went in unto her. ²⁴And Laban gave unto his daughter Leah Zilpah his maid for an handmaid. ²⁵And it came to pass, that in the morning, behold, it was Leah: and he said to Laban, What is this thou hast done unto me? did not I serve with thee for Rachel? wherefore then hast thou beguiled me? ²⁶And Laban said, It must not be so done in our country, to give the younger before the firstborn. ²⁷Fulfil her week, and we will give thee this also for the service which thou shalt serve with me yet seven other years. ²⁸And Jacob did so, and fulfilled her week: and he gave him Rachel his daughter to wife also. ²⁹And Laban gave to Rachel his daughter Bilhah his handmaid to be her maid. ³⁰And he went in also unto Rachel, and he loved also Rachel more than Leah,* and served with him yet seven other years. *³¹* And when the LORD saw that Leah was hated, he opened her womb: but Rachel was barren. *³²* And Leah conceived, and bare a son, and she called his name Reuben: for she said, Surely the LORD hath looked upon my affliction; now therefore my husband will love me. *³³* And she conceived again, and bare a son; and said, Because the LORD hath heard I was hated, he hath therefore given me this son also: and she called his name Simeon. *³⁴* And she conceived again, and bare a son; and said, Now this time will my husband be joined unto me, because I have born him three sons: therefore was his name called Levi. *³⁵* And she conceived again, and bare a son: and she said, Now will I praise the LORD: therefore she called his name Judah; and left bearing.

Genesis 30:1-25: *¹* And when Rachel saw that she bare Jacob no children, Rachel envied her sister; and said unto Jacob, Give me children, or else I die. *²* And Jacob's anger was kindled against Rachel: and he said, Am I in God's stead, who hath withheld from thee the fruit of the womb? *³* And she said, Behold my maid Bilhah, go in unto her; and she shall bear upon my knees, that I may also have children by her. *⁴* And she gave him Bilhah her handmaid to wife: and Jacob went in unto her. *⁵* And Bilhah conceived, and bare Jacob a son. *⁶* And Rachel said, God hath judged me, and hath also heard my voice, and hath given me a son: therefore called she his name Dan. *⁷* And Bilhah Rachel's maid conceived again, and bare Jacob a second son. *⁸* And Rachel said, With great wrestlings have I wrestled with my sister, and I have prevailed: and she called his name Naphtali. *⁹* When Leah saw that she had left bearing, she took Zilpah her maid, and gave her Jacob to wife. *¹⁰* And Zilpah Leah's maid bare Jacob a son. *¹¹* And Leah said, A troop cometh: and she called his name Gad. *¹²* And Zilpah

Leah's maid bare Jacob a second son. *¹³ And Leah said, Happy am I, for the daughters will call me blessed: and she called his name Asher. ¹⁴ And Reuben went in the days of wheat harvest, and found mandrakes in the field, and brought them unto his mother Leah. Then Rachel said to Leah, Give me, I pray thee, of thy son's mandrakes. ¹⁵ And she said unto her, Is it a small matter that thou hast taken my husband? and wouldest thou take away my son's mandrakes also? And Rachel said, Therefore he shall lie with thee to night for thy son's mandrakes. ¹⁶ And Jacob came out of the field in the evening, and Leah went out to meet him, and said, Thou must come in unto me; for surely I have hired thee with my son's mandrakes. And he lay with her that night. ¹⁷ And God hearkened unto Leah, and she conceived, and bare Jacob the fifth son. ¹⁸ And Leah said, God hath given me my hire, because I have given my maiden to my husband: and she called his name Issachar. ¹⁹ And Leah conceived again, and bare Jacob the sixth son. ²⁰ And Leah said, God hath endued me with a good dowry; now will my husband dwell with me, because I have born him six sons: and she called his name Zebulun. ²¹ And afterwards she bare a daughter, and called her name Dinah. ²² And God remembered Rachel, and God hearkened to her, and opened her womb. ²³ And she conceived, and bare a son; and said, God hath taken away my reproach: ²⁴ And she called his name Joseph; and said, The* LORD *shall add to me another son. ²⁵ And it came to pass, when Rachel had born Joseph, that Jacob said unto Laban, Send me away, that I may go unto mine own place, and to my country.*

Genesis 35:16-20: *¹⁶ And they journeyed from Bethel; and there was but a little way to come to Ephrath: and Rachel travailed, and she had hard labour. ¹⁷ And it came to pass, when she was in hard labour, that the midwife said unto her, Fear not; thou shalt have this son also.*

¹⁸ And it came to pass, as her soul was in departing, (for she died) that she called his name Benoni: but his father called him Benjamin. ¹⁹ And Rachel died, and was buried in the way to Ephrath, which is Bethlehem. ²⁰ And Jacob set a pillar upon her grave: that is the pillar of Rachel's grave unto this day.

INTRODUCTION

The story of Jacob's Desperate Housewives of Biblical Proportions: Leah, Bilhah, Zilpah and Rachel

In the life of Jacob who later is renamed Israel, we see his life, his version of love, his influence in and upon his wives and children and how their actions impacted the entire nation of Israel. Take a journey with me as we take a deep dive into the lives of Leah, Rachel, Zilpah and Bilhah. Our very own Desperate Housewives to one (1) husband, Jacob (Israel), and their lifelong fight to be seen, loved and appreciated. We will see how their actions, feelings and thoughts play out in the lives of the children in this dysfunctional yet divinely favored family. To understand Jacob's desperate housewives, we must first get to know the patriarch. Jacob is one of the twin sons born to Isaac and Rebekah and the grandson of Abraham and Sarah who tricked his fraternal twin brother, Esau, out of his birthright, and deceived his blind and ailing father, Isaac, into receiving the blessing that belonged to Esau as the first born son. Jacob is said to have had 12 sons and one (1) daughter by four (4) women, his desperate housewives: Leah and Rachel and his concubines: Bilhah and Zilpah. Jacob is known to display favoritism among his wives and children, preferring Rachel and her sons (Joseph and Benjamin) causing tension within the family, and culminating in the sale of Joseph by his brothers into slavery. Let me slow down before I get ahead of myself. Let's begin at Jacob's request to marry Rachel in Genesis 29:13-30.

Laban instructed Jacob to work for him seven (7) years to marry Rachel, however, Laban deceives Jacob and gave Leah as Jacob's wife with the excuse, "...*it must not be so done in our country, to give the younger before the firstborn.*" This caused Jacob to work an additional seven (7) years for Laban to marry Rachel. This one (1) act solidified Leah's position in Jacob's life, heart and home, and created a deeper sense of comparison and desire to be loved for Leah. Why? Because Leah knew Jacob didn't love her and in some regards she felt Jacob hated her because she was the instrument Laban used to deceive Jacob and force him to work an additional seven (7) years to marry the love of his life, Rachel. As they say, it's on! The competition has begun to win Jacob's affection and to find favor in his eyes between Leah and Rachel. This is where our story begins with Jacob beginning his life married to Rachel and having no love for Leah only a sense of responsibility and/or commitment. Well, let me clear that up he's committed to caring for her and having children with her, but not in loving her as described by God, "...*Husbands, love your wives, even as Christ also loved the church, and gave himself for it...*" (Ephesians 5:25)

LEAH
(Weary)

SCRIPTURE LESSON: Genesis 29: 13-35 (KJV). *"And it came to pass, when Laban heard the tidings of Jacob his sister's son, that he ran to meet him, and embraced him, and kissed him, and brought him to his house. And he told Laban all these things. And Laban said to him, Surely, thou art my bone and my flesh. And he abode with him the space of a month. And Laban said unto Jacob, because thou art my brother, shouldest thou therefore serve me for nought? tell me, what shall thy wages be? And Laban had two daughters: the name of the elder was Leah, and the name of the younger was Rachel. Leah was tender eyed; but Rachel was beautiful and well favoured. And Jacob loved Rachel; and said, I will serve thee seven years for Rachel thy younger daughter. And Laban said, it is better that I give her to thee, than that I should give her to another man: abide with me. And Jacob served seven years for Rachel; and they seemed unto him but a few days, for the love he had to her. And Jacob said unto Laban, give me my wife, for my days are fulfilled, that I may go in unto her. And Laban gathered together all the men of the place and made a feast. And it came to pass in the evening, that he took Leah his daughter, and brought her to him; and he went in unto her. And Laban gave unto his daughter Leah Zilpah his maid for a handmaid. And it came to pass, that in the morning, behold, it was Leah: and he said to Laban, What is this thou hast done unto me? did not I serve with thee for Rachel? wherefore then hast thou beguiled me? And Laban said, it must not be so done in our country, to give the younger* *before the firstborn. Fulfil her week, and we will give thee this also for the service which thou shalt serve with me yet seven other years. And Jacob did so and fulfilled her week: and he gave him Rachel his daughter to wife also. And Laban gave to Rachel his daughter Bilhah his handmaid to be her maid. And he went in also unto Rachel, and he loved also Rachel more than Leah, and served with him yet seven other years. And when the Lord saw that Leah was hated, he opened her womb: but Rachel was barren. And Leah conceived, and bare a son, and she called his name Reuben: for she said, Surely the Lord hath looked upon my affliction; now therefore my husband will love me. And she conceived again, and bare a son; and said, Because the Lord hath heard I was hated, he hath therefore given me this son also: and she called his name Simeon. And she conceived again, and bare a son; and said, now this time will my husband be joined unto me, because I have born him three sons: therefore, was his name called Levi. And she conceived again, and bare a son: and she said, now will I praise the Lord: therefore, she called his name Judah; and left bearing."*

HISTORICAL ANALYSIS: Leah is the first-born daughter to Laban and Adanah. The Bible describes Leah as having "tender eyes." There's much controversy which definition the description refers to, her eyes being "delicate and soft" or "weary.' Rabbinic interpretation speaks to Laban having two (2) daughters: Leah and Rachel and his sister, Rebekah, having two (2) sons: Esau and Jacob. It says that the older son of Rebekah, Esau, was to marry the older daughter of Laban, Leah, and the younger son, Jacob, was to marry Laban's younger daughter, Rachel. Being made aware of this, Leah spent most of her time weeping and praying to

God to change her destined mate. Why? Because Esau was a "man of the field," who became a hunter who had rough qualities that distinguished him from his fraternal twin brother. The most notable of Esau's qualities were his red hair and overall hairiness. In this we see that Leah believed in God and was caught up in the same things we are today, the look of the man and not the heart of the man. Because of Leah's continuous crying out to God, God heard her prayers and was touched by her tears. He allowed her to be Jacob's first wife, but it came at a cost! A cost that exacted a price that left Leah feeling unloved and even sometimes hated by her husband. As the saying goes "...*be careful what you wish for, you may get more than you bargained for...*"

In Genesis 1:27-28, we find marriage ordained by God with the instruction for the man and the woman to "...*be fruitful and multiply, fill the earth and subdue it.*"

In Bible days women were promised in marriage almost from birth to solidify family relations, to build or maintain a family's prestige and/or lineage. The women and all they possessed became the property or possession of their husband to do with as he sees fit. The woman's identity is formed by her relationship with her husband and her ability to produce children and not just any children but male children. In the article *"Biblical Marriage Unmasked,"* (www.believeoutloud.com) it says, "*A woman's dignity and worth as one created in the image of God is subordinated to the needs and desire of the man... women are often equated with a house or livestock (Deut.*

20:5-7)." Considering the custom of the day, very few marriages were because of love. They were business deals that were cemented on the wedding night in the wedding chamber. This may shed some light on the significance of why Laban deceived Jacob and forced him to work for him an additional seven (7) years to marry the love of his life, Rachel.

Imagine how you'd feel if after a week of marital bliss your husband takes another wife. Not just any wife but your sister; your little sister. That one act had the ability to force you back to reality and the knowledge that your relationship amounted to nothing more than a business deal as you continue to compare yourself to your beautiful little sister.

LET THE GAMES BEGIN: Leah is forced to realize that even though God answered her prayers, she's now married to a man who does not love her. As a matter of fact, he's in love with her little sister, which in and of itself is a bittersweet pill for Leah to swallow. Because of this God opened Leah's womb, and she becomes pregnant with a son. A son she names, Reuben. Leah shows her mental and emotional condition, as well as her heart condition in the meaning of **Reuben**'s name, "*…the Lord has noticed my misery, and now my husband will love me.*" This trend continues in the naming of the other children born to her. Leah gave birth to her 2nd son, **Simeon**, whose name means "*…the Lord heard that I was unloved and has given me another son.*" Leah became pregnant a third time and gave birth to another son, **Levi**, whose name means "*...surely this time my husband will feel affection for me, since I have given him three (3) sons.*" Once again Leah became pregnant and gave birth to her fourth son, **Judah**, whose name means "*...now I will praise the Lord.*"

PARENTHETICAL CITATION: What Leah failed to realize is that one of her sons would be the forefather of the tribe in which the promised Messiah would come through (Genesis 49:9–12; Matthew 2:6; Hebrews 7:14; Revelation 5:5). Sometimes what we see as difficult and unbearable is what God uses to bless generations to come because of our willingness to endure even in the face of adversity. Through my Christian journey I have often heard that "*...God gives His toughest battles to His strongest soldiers.*" At the time that this was said to me I did not see it or feel it, and I am sure if someone had said this to Leah, she wouldn't have seen it or felt it either. Why? Because she could only see what she could see and feel what she could feel in the moment. You know, what was her reality at that moment: finding herself being compared to her sister (even if only in her own head), feeling unloved and her husband favoring her little sister, his second wife, Rachel.

LEAH'S LOW SELF ESTEEM: Earlier in the book, I alluded to the Desperate Housewives all having a relationship with barrenness that is represented in their personal description of themselves. Although Leah is not childless, she is experiencing barrenness at its most primal meaning which is defined as being empty of meaning or value; devoid of. This is significant in Leah's story because she finds herself in a loveless marriage with a man who is in love with another woman. Leah's inability to gain or even steal her husband's love from his other wife, her sister, Rachel, is directly related to her current barren situation. Jacob's inability to simply see Leah, her needs and offer the unconditional love she desperately desires leaves Leah feeling empty of meaning and value, and devoid of the love she so desperately desires causing her feelings of unworthiness which is directly related to her low self-value and/or self-esteem.

"Self-esteem is a confidence in one's own worth or abilities. Therefore, low self-esteem is a lack of confidence in one's own abilities and a bad feeling about oneself. It can be caused by: (1) dwelling on your flaws: this is as a result of being conscious of your flaws and weaknesses; and/or (2) taking the negative words people say about you to heart. Leah felt she was married to Jacob because custom demanded that the eldest daughter was to get married before the younger and not because he chose her or loved her. However, Jacob chose to marry Rachel (though she was the younger daughter and her elder sister was unmarried) instead of Leah because he found the desired qualities he wanted in Rachel. Leah had her own beautiful qualities and abilities and there was a man who could have loved her for her own abilities if she was not given to Jacob based on tradition. The sad part of this story is the fact that Leah did not discover her qualities and abilities and could not be confident in herself, but instead dwelt on her flaws and had the notion that her sister was better than her, which was one of the reasons her husband could not love her. ("Low Self-Esteem, by Okoh Michael Damilola): https://agfchurchs.org/low-self-esteem/.

Psychiatrist, Dr. Nathaniel Branden, says *"No factor is more important in people's psychological development and motivation than the value judgments they make about themselves. Every aspect of their lives is impacted by the way they see themselves."* Although Dr. Branden made this statement years after Leah's death, it was as if he was speaking specifically about the mental and emotional state that followed Leah daily in the same way that a shadow follows an individual. It is even evident in the fact that Leah was unable to celebrate the blessing of birthing children and experience the love and joy that overflows from the heart when first looking upon the face of the new baby she just birthed. It is apparent in Leah's comments that she has spent a lifetime being compared to her sister, Rachel, and being found lacking each and every time. Leah seemed to accept the negative comments and after some time began to wear it as a cloak and/or badge of honor. As if this is something to be proud of and to think towards herself. Leah failed to look within for what she desired, but continuously set herself up for failure by looking to Jacob to give her something he is incapable of giving her. Jacob is a product of a dysfunctional home where favoritism was the norm. By keeping that in mind, we can better understand why Jacob was incapable of giving Leah what she needed because he had already invested all he was capable of giving in Rachel. The woman he chose and not the wife of deception.

As they say the proof is in the pudding, and in Leah's case that pudding was reflected in the names Leah gave to each of her sons that speak of her low self-esteem. Leah birthed each one (1) from a place of hurt, disillusionment, desperation and rejection, and never realized the impact that her beginning had in setting the tone for her relationship with Jacob. In Leah's mind it proved that she was a continual reminder of Laban's deception, and the reason why Jacob could not love, cherish and respect her. As I am being a willing spectator of Leah's journey, Matthew 12:34 comes to mind, "...*out of the abundance of the heart the mouth speaks.*" Many women throughout time have found themselves in a "Leah situation." Stuck in a loveless marriage to a husband who is too caught up in his own desires and needs to give them the one (1) thing they desire and crave, LOVE, the unconditional kind. Sometimes their sense of duty to provide for their family keeps them blind to the fact that women were created out of the love God has for man and as such it is needed to help her grow fully into her own as a devoted wife, mother and woman (Genesis 2:18-25).

Jacob's inability to give Leah what she most desired and wanted, left her to speak that insecurity and unloved status into the hearts and minds of her sons. According to GoodTherapy.com "...*when parental involvement is limited, children typically receive scant mirroring or encouragement. They have no one reflecting back to them that they are worthwhile, admirable or interesting... Without the experience of parents responding to a child's spirit and achievements (whether taking first steps, laughing at their jokes, making a diorama or going on a first date) children are deprived of the building blocks for self-confidence and self-esteem. To feel "I can do it," or even more important, "You are proud, pleased and delighted with me," is a crucial experience…" for any child.* It goes on to say, *"A parent's pleasure at a child's achievements and with the person becomes a platform from which a child ventures out into the world with the knowledge that he or she will be ok… this balance between providing support and giving children the freedom to discover their own individual desires, strengths and weaknesses is the basis of how children, develop self-confidence and self-esteem."*

With that being said, we can clearly see the correlation of this in Leah's life: the constant comparison between her and Rachel during her childhood and now during her marriage. The words no longer had to be said, they are committed to memory in her heart and in her mind. The thoughts of how everyone equated Rachel with beauty and how her father, Laban, used her to force Jacob into working for him an additional seven (7) years for his own selfish reasons and desires. This is also played out in the lives of Esau and Jacob and in how Isaac favored Esau and Rebekah favored Jacob. In their lives as well as in their genetic make-up we find Esau constantly looking for approval and Jacob finding favorites within his own lineage which brought about dissention and strife among his children. Add in Leah's issues and we find ourselves seeing a dysfunctional family operating with their insecurities leading them. Instead of operating despite them.

Genesis 30:14-21: *[14] And Reuben went in the days of wheat harvest, and found mandrakes in the field, and brought them unto his mother Leah. Then Rachel said to Leah, Give me, I pray thee, of thy son's* mandrakes. *¹⁵ And she said unto her, Is it a small matter that thou hast taken my husband? and wouldest thou take away my son's mandrakes also? And Rachel said, Therefore he shall lie with thee to night for thy son's mandrakes. ¹⁶ And Jacob came out of the field in the evening, and Leah went out to meet him, and said, Thou must come in unto me; for surely I have hired thee with my son's mandrakes. And he lay with her that night. ¹⁷ And God hearkened unto Leah, and she conceived, and bare Jacob the fifth son. ¹⁸ And Leah said, God hath given me my hire, because I have given my maiden to my husband: and she called his name Issachar. ¹⁹ And Leah conceived again, and bare Jacob the sixth son. ²⁰ And Leah said, God hath endued me with a good dowry; now will my husband dwell with me, because I have born him six sons: and she called his name Zebulun. ²¹ And afterwards she bare a daughter, and called her name Dinah.*

THE MANDRAKES: The competition continued between Leah and Rachel in which I am sure that Jacob grew tired of hearing about and seeing play out before his very eyes that seemed to continue without an end in sight. After the two (2) sons that Leah's handmaid bares Jacob, we find Leah using an innocent find to her own benefit. Leah's oldest son Reuben brought in mandrake plants from the field and Rachel found out and demanded he give them to her. Rachel believed that mandrakes would counter infertility (barrenness). In an article from April 24, 2011 on *"God as Gardner: Fertility and Mandrake,"* describes the mandrake scenario as, *"The story of the mandrakes began with Leah's oldest son, Reuben, finding mandrake plants in the field and bringing mandrake roots to Leah. Rachel saw the plants and asked Leah for* *them. Resentful of Jacob's preference for Rachel, Leah asked Rachel, "Wasn't it enough that you took away my husband? Will you take my son's mandrakes too?" Rachel responded by proposing a trade – Jacob can sleep with Leah that night in return for the mandrakes. Leah agreed. When Jacob came in from the fields, he was met by Leah who said, "You must sleep with me. I have hired you with my son's mandrakes." …Rachel did not become pregnant as a result of acquiring – and most likely using – the mandrakes from Leah."* This statement leads me to believe that Leah saw the exchange as an opportunity to strike up a deal with Rachel and to get Jacob out of Rachel's bed and tent.

Let's take a deeper dive into this one act! For Leah to make this agreement with Rachel it leads one to believe that Jacob spent most his nighttime hours in Rachel's bed and tent.

Remember he loved and favored Rachel above all else, that included Leah. I find it interesting that there is no reference of further conversation between Rachel and Jacob about how she would agree to such a thing. Jacob knew of Rachel's desperation to have a child of her own and to satisfy her he went along with the agreement. Which shows you that Jacob saw this as a win-win situation. Leah has always been fertile and laying with her may produce more sons and with Rachel eating the mandrakes it very well may reverse her barrenness and open her womb for her to conceive. Unlike Leah, Rachel failed to put her trust in God to open her womb and began to seek other measures to get the job done. So, Jacob lays with Leah and Leah conceives and bares Jacob a fifth son: **Issachar** whose name means "*...my hire or reward.*" It is as if Leah was thanking God for blessing her with this fifth son because "*...she gave her handmaid to Jacob as a wife/concubine.*" After that Leah conceived again and bore Jacob a sixth son, Zebulon whose name means *dwelling or cohabitation*. According to the scriptures, Leah concluded that "*...God hath endued me with a good dowry; now will my husband dwell with me, because I have born him six sons...*" (Genesis 30:19-20). The next child born to Leah and Jacob is a daughter, Dinah. Dinah means vindicated. Leah believed that "*...God was vindicating her in the struggle with Rachel over Jacob's affections.*" Leah's own words spoke to her competition with Rachel and her feeling that she is better than Rachel in that regard. As the sub-title suggests, comparison kills. It kills the person doing the comparison and the object of the comparison. In this case, it killed the loving and supportive familial relationship and the sisterhood bond that Leah and Rachel should've and/or could've had.

I submit that God purposefully redirected Leah's attention when He determined it was time to open Rachel's womb when He allowed Leah to have one (1) more child: a daughter to focus on raising and passing down their traditions to. A daughter she could pour into to take away some of the sting she'd experience when Rachel began conceiving and baring Jacob's children. Dinah may have meant *vindication* to Leah, but I surmise she was the object God used to redirect Leah's attention away from Rachel and her competition with her. Simply put God redirected her desperation into purpose. She was tasked with preparing Dinah to be a wife and mother, and an active participant in the continuation of their traditions.

LEAH'S DEATH: In Genesis 49:31, we find that Leah died some time before Jacob and is believed to be buried in the Cave of the Patriarchs in Hebron alongside Jacob. It is also believed that this cave houses the graves of Abraham and Sarah and Isaac and Rebekah. It's as if Leah found in death what she desperately desired in life; to be with her husband in a place of honor that solidified her place as Jacob's wife and represents the love and acceptance she has always desired to have from him.

BILHAH
(to wear out, annul or use until worthlessness; unworried)

SCRIPTURE LESSON: Genesis 30: 1-8 (KJV). *"And when Rachel saw that she bare Jacob no children, Rachel envied her sister; and said unto Jacob, Give me children, or else I die. ²And Jacob's anger was kindled against Rachel: and he said, Am I in God's stead, who hath withheld from thee the fruit of the womb? ³And she said, Behold my maid Bilhah, go in unto her; and she shall bear upon my knees, that I may also have children by her. ⁴And she gave him Bilhah her handmaid to wife: and Jacob went in unto her. ⁵And Bilhah conceived, and bore Jacob a son. ⁶And Rachel said, God hath judged me, and hath also heard my voice, and hath given me a son: therefore, called she his name Dan. ⁷And Bilhah Rachel's maid conceived again, and bare Jacob a second son. ⁸And Rachel said, With great wrestling's have I wrestled with my sister, and I have prevailed: and she called his name Naphtali."*

HISTORICAL ANALYSIS: Bilhah is the daughter of Rotheus and Euna and the older sister to Zilpah (Leah's handmaid). Bilhah was given to Rachel by Laban as a handmaid upon Rachel's marriage to Jacob. Bilhah is a Hebrew name meaning to wear out, annul or use until worthlessness according to www.abarim-publications.com, however, in Wikipedia it means unworried. Although Bilhah is on the scene serving Rachel it isn't until Genesis 30:3 that Bilhah comes out of the shadows and begins to play a major role as one of the main characters in our story, the Desperate Housewives of Biblical Proportions.

RACHEL'S SURROGATE: Rachel presents Bilhah to Jacob that "...*she may bear upon my knees, that I may also have children by her.*" (Genesis 30:3) This is the second time in the Bible that a wife provides a surrogate to have children in her place (Sarai is the first, Genesis 16:1-4). This speaks to Rachel's desperation to have children to give her handmaid (her slave) to her husband to produce children for her. Previously, I mentioned that Rachel gave Bilhah to Jacob as a concubine or a pilegesh. (A concubine in the Jewish tradition is a woman with similar social and legal standing to a recognized wife. However, Bilhah is not formerly identified as Jacob's concubine until in Genesis 35:22.) Jacob accepted Bilhah as a concubine, and she bore him two (2) sons. Rachel named the first son, **Dan**, meaning "...*God has vindicated me! He has heard my request and given me a son.*" Rachel names the second son born to Bilhah, **Naphtali**, meaning "...*I have struggled with my sister, and I am winning.*" As we saw with Leah, we find Rachel in competition with Leah which in turn causes the two (2) sons born to Bilhah to be the casualties of their rivalry.

That isn't the end of the story for Bilhah. We find that Leah's eldest son, Reuben, goes in and lays with his father's concubine while his father is away (Genesis 35:22). As a result of this adultery, Reuben lost the respect of his father. According to Wikipedia, "...*some rabbinical commentators interpreted the story differently, saying that Reuben's disruption of Bilhah's and Jacob's beds was not through sex with Bilhah. As long as Rachel was alive, it is believed that Jacob kept his bed in Rachel's tent and visited the other wives in their individual tents. However, when Rachel died, Jacob moved his bed into the tent of Bilhah, who had been mentored by Rachel to retain a closeness to his favorite wife. Reuben, Leah's eldest, felt that this move slighted his mother, who was also a primary wife, and so Reuben took it upon himself to move Jacob's bed into his mother's tent and removed or overturned Bilhah's"* (a sign of disrespect). This is considered to be a mahloket (disagreement) in the Talmud. According to *"The Bible Says What? 'Reuben slept with his father's concubine,'"* (*www.jewishnews.timesofisrael.com*) by Rabbi Elana Dellal, January 17, 2020, *"Some argue that Reuben did in fact lay with Bilhah and was deserving of his punishment. We can't know what really happened, but it is interesting, though unsurprising, that we never hear Bilhah's account of the incident* (keep in mind the meaning of her name) *…Nor do we hear her perspective or voice when she lends her womb to Rachel to support her and Jacob's relationship when they are struggling with infertility. The silence of Bilhah, like so many other Torah narratives of women, speaks volumes about the marginalization of women within the Jewish customs."* What is abundantly clear is that the invasion of Jacob's privacy was viewed as adultery in the Bible and resulted in Reuben losing his first-born right to a double inheritance (Genesis 49:1-4).

Bilhah isn't mentioned anymore nor is there any evidence that Jacob/Israel fathered additional children with her. It is as if after Reuben's disrespectful actions, Jacob no longer viewed Bilhah as a surrogate for his beloved Rachel, but as damaged or used goods. It is as if her worth to him had diminished in his eyes. I am sure this made her feel worthless especially since she bore him two (2) sons that became a part of the Abrahamic covenant.

ZILPAH
(uncertain)

SCRIPTURE LESSON: Genesis 30: 9-13 (KJV). *⁹When Leah saw that she had left bearing, she took Zilpah her maid, and gave her Jacob to wife. ¹⁰And Zilpah Leah's maid bare Jacob a son. ¹¹And Leah said, A troop cometh: and she called his name Gad. ¹²And Zilpah Leah's maid bare Jacob a second son. ¹³And Leah said, Happy am I, for the daughters will call me blessed: and she called his name Asher.*

HISTORICAL ANALYSIS: Zilpah is the daughter of Rotheus and Euna and the younger sister to Bilhah (Rachel's handmaid). Zilpah is a Hebrew word that means 'to trickle or youthful' according to the Strong's Old Testament Hebrew Lexicon, however in Wikipedia it means 'uncertain'. Zilpah was given to Leah by her father, Laban, on her wedding day as a handmaid and it is speculated that both Zilpah and Bilhah are younger daughters of Laban born by one of his wives/concubines, Euna, that is later given to Rotheus. This definitely speaks to the culture in which Zilpah was raised and speaks of it being customary for men to have more than one (1) wife and how women are treated like property, which seems to be the case for Laban.

LEAH'S SURROGATE: When Leah realizes she has stopped bearing children, she takes a page out of Rachel's and Sarah's handbooks and gives her handmaid, Zilpah, to Jacob as wife number four (4) (or 2nd concubine). Zilpah in turn bore

Jacob two (2) sons who Leah named Gad and Asher. **Gad**'s name means *a troop cometh*, as if this one added to Leah's other four (4) sons would make a "trooper", an army (Genesis 30:11). Zilpah lays with Jacob again and conceives a second son, whom Leah names **Asher** whose name means *happiness or blessedness*. Leah believed that "…*women would call her happy and blessed because of the six (6) sons borne to Jacob by her and her handmaid, Zilpah.*" (Genesis 30:12) Every move we see Leah make is so that she's seen in a certain light even though it isn't how she sees or feels about herself. Then to bring Zilpah into this madness and this act of desperation shows us Zilpah's willingness to be a vessel that Leah uses to get what she believes she wants: acceptance, love and approval. To what lengths will women go to get what they perceive they need when they act in desperation.

Although Zilpah is believed to have had additional children with Israel, there is no concrete information to support this statement in the Bible. It is believed that Zilpah continued to serve both Leah, as her handmaid, and Jacob, as his concubine, until their deaths.

RACHEL
(ewe; female sheep; princess)

SCRIPTURE LESSON: Genesis 30:22-24 (KJV). *[22] And God remembered Rachel, and God hearkened to her, and opened her womb. [23] And she conceived, and bare a son; and said, God hath taken away my reproach: [24] And she called his name Joseph; and said, The LORD shall add to me another son.* **Genesis 35:16-20** (KJV). *[16] And they journeyed from Bethel; and there was but a little way to come to Ephrath: and Rachel travailed, and she had hard labour. [17] And it came to pass, when she was in hard labour, that the midwife said unto her, Fear not; thou shalt have this son also. [18] And it came to pass, as her soul was in departing, (for she died) that she called his name Benoni: but his father called him Benjamin. [19] And Rachel died, and was buried in the way to Ephrath, which is Bethlehem. [20] And Jacob set a pillar upon her grave: that is the pillar of Rachel's grave unto this day.*

HISTORICAL ANALYSIS: Rachel is the youngest daughter born to Laban and Adinah, and the younger sister to Leah. Rachel was responsible for helping with the family business, sheep herding. Her first reference in the Bible is in Genesis chapter 29 when she is about to water her father's flock. Rachel is described as *"lovely in form and beautiful"* to her sister's description of having *"tender eyes."* In the Jewish family the first born holds a special place within the family especially if it is a male. Now remember in Bible days women did not have rights and were considered property.

When they married, regardless of their role in the family, any property they may have had reverts to their husband for him to do with as he so chooses.

Rachel as the younger daughter had less opportunities available to her and is why in Genesis 29, we find her at the well preparing to water the sheep. It was the same as any other day except she saw the man of her dreams and the man she hoped to one day marry. Now, we did not discuss customs in Leah's chapter, however, in the Jewish custom marriages are arranged normally at birth and are not a part of a love selection process. As discussed in Leah's chapter, Rachel had been promised to Jacob if things would have gone as planned, but because of Laban's deception, Esau having taken wives from the Canaanite nation and Laban's desire to marry off his eldest daughter first and his greediness, Rachel had to sit back and watch the love of her life marry her big sister. Although she knew she would one day marry Jacob, she had to wait until a week past of Leah sharing Jacob's wedding/marriage bed before she could call him husband. And, if that is not enough, she has to share him with her sister for as long as she lived. I do not know about you but that is akin to adding insult to injury.

RACHEL'S REPROACH: In the 30th chapter of Genesis we find Rachel experiencing a feeling that is new to her, jealousy. Now that Rachel and Jacob are married, Rachel is been forced to watch Leah birth son after son to Jacob while she is barren. In Genesis 30:1, Rachel says to Jacob "...*give* *me children or else I die.*" This statement angers Jacob and causes him to verbally lash out to her while asking "*Am I God?*" What Rachel did not see is that she, Sarah and Rebekah were plagued with the same issue, barrenness. According to Tikva Frymar-Kensky "*The infertility of the matriarchs has two (2) effects: it heightens the drama of the birth of the eventual son as special; and it emphasizes that pregnancy is an act of God.*" Which reiterated how the Jews saw barrenness as a mark of divine displeasure. Knowing you are barren and accepting it is two (2) vastly different things because you also accept the shame that accompanies it. It is only when Rachel accepts her barren condition that she steps into the realization that she can have a surrogate and offers her handmaid, Bilhah, to Jacob and says, "*…go in unto her; and she shall bear upon my knees that I may also have children by her.*" Rachel followed Sarai's actions found in Genesis 16:2. Sarai, Rachel's grandmother-in-law did the very same thing when she offered Hagar, her slave woman, as a concubine to her husband, Abram, so that he might have a child. In desperation Sarai stepped outside of God's promise to Abram because she could not see it happening, otherwise. Once Hagar conceived the dynamic in the household changed due to Sarai's jealousy resulting in the deterioration of her relationship with Hagar. Just as was discussed in the introduction, we see, in this family dynamic, the "*domestic struggles and family life… in their beautiful and seemingly perfect* *lives."* This just proves once again that *"…everything that glitters ain't gold."*

By offering her handmaid to Jacob, Rachel did as Sarai had taught and offered Bilhah as her surrogate to have children for her. That offering resulted in Bilhah baring Jacob two (2) sons who Rachel named Dan and Naphtali. Although Jacob is committed to Rachel and loves her above all else; (in her eyes) she believed that her place in the family was not cemented especially if she did not provide Jacob with any children, specifically a male child.

Let's take a closer look at Rachel and what she is dealing with as a barren woman. In an article on www.NewScientist.com titled *"Infertility may increase risk of mental disorders"* by Tiffany O'Callaghan on July 5, 2012 that says, *"Not being able to have children when you desperately want them can be understandably stressful. It is known that this experience can lead to anxiety and depression."* In an article published on *www.health.harvard.edu*, titled *"The psychological impact of infertility and its treatments,"* May 2009 says, *"..women with infertility felt as anxious or depressed as those diagnosed with cancer, hypertension or recovering from a heart attack."* It went on to say, *"…typical reactions include shock, grief, depression, anger and frustration, as well as a loss of self-esteem, self-confidence and a sense of control over one's destiny."* The women in Bible days didn't have the opportunities to have children due to their barrenness as we do today. They were silent suffers of both emotional and mental pain as well as shame and in some cases being publicly ostracized by their peers for not being able to birth a child, specifically a male child. If nothing else this should give you a clearer picture of why in desperation Rachel said to Jacob, "...*give me children, or I'll die...*" It was as if the tables were turned on Rachel and she was now personally seeing what Leah dealt with while living in Rachel's shadow. She was experiencing the mental, emotional, and social pain of being barren. It is as if she was Cinderella in reverse, she was the Belle of the Ball only to become the invisible servant.

JEWISHNESS: In Bible times, although women were considered second class citizens and/or property they still played a major role in the Jewish family. According to Wikipedia, the role of women in Judaism is determined by the Hebrew Bible, the oral law, by custom(s) and by cultural factors. In traditional Judaism, Jewishness (*answers a basic question about one's Jewish identity*) is passed down through the mother (*if she is Jewish or has undergone a halokhic conversion*), even though the father's name is used to describe their sons and daughters (i.e. Dinah daughter of Jacob).

THE STRUGGLE IS REAL: As I sit here contemplating Rachel's struggle with infertility, her relationship with barrenness and her seemingly fall from grace, I am stunned at the magnitude of desperation she exhibits. I am forced to go back to the Biblical description of Rachel. It says "*...Rachel was beautiful and well favoured.*" According to the King James Bible Dictionary, beautiful is defined as elegant in form, fair, having the form that pleases the eye (aesthetically beautiful) and favoured means a feature, countenance. In everything I have read about Rachel it speaks of her outward beauty and nothing of her inward beauty: her personality or character. It isn't until difficulty enters her life that we begin to see her mask of beauty begin to crack. As we take a bird's eye view, we begin to see how her favored life begins to unravel as the realization hits that the life of privilege she's accustomed to no longer exists because her beautiful body has literally turned against her. This same body that has afforded her privileges not available to her sister, Leah, the body that has been the tool used to compare her to her sister and has left Leah feeling inadequate, and the body that has made Rachel feel superior to those less fortunate people who aren't seen as beautiful, will not do the one (1) thing she's been waiting her whole life to experience, have a child.

When faced with this fact and reality, Rachel's true character begins to present itself. The side of her that isn't to be seen in polite, let alone, mixed company. We find three (3) specific instances where Rachel's character does not reflect the beautiful exterior she presents to the world daily: 1) Rachel steals Laban's idol gods (Genesis 31:30-35), hides them and then lies about her current physical condition to keep them hidden; 2) when Rachel becomes envious of her sister Leah (Genesis 30:1); and 3) when Rachel demands of Jacob to "...*give her children or else I die.*" (Genesis 30:1). In each of the aforementioned items, we see Rachel experiencing feelings foreign to her and feelings she is unprepared and ill equipped to handle. Some Bible scholars say that Rachel begins dealing with depression and/or anxiety because there is apparently nothing that can be done to rectify her current struggle with infertility. According to the Harvard Mental Health Letter article entitled, *The psychological impact of infertility and its treatment (www.health.harvard.edu/newsletter_article/The-psychological-impact-of-infertility-and-its-treatment),* Published: May, 2009), *"...Individuals who learn they are infertile often experience the normal but nevertheless distressing emotions common to those who are grieving any significant loss — in this case the ability to procreate. Typical reactions include shock, grief, depression, anger, and frustration, as well as loss of self-esteem, self-confidence, and a sense of control over one's destiny. Relationships may suffer — not only the primary relationship with a spouse or partner, but also those with friends and family members who may inadvertently cause pain by offering well-meaning but misguided opinions and advice."*

Like Rachel, many people have had their character judged negatively because of their actions, behaviors and/or decisions/choices. They have found that people don't want to be around them because of their bad attitude and/or their nasty disposition, even if they are aware of the reason why they are acting negatively. As we get to know Rachel and her struggles, we see a woman who is lost because life isn't happening as expected. Struggles that leave her feeling alienated from her familial community, alienated from the love of her life and alienated from the honor of having children and taking her rightful place within the family. As stated in the excerpt from the article in the Harvard Mental Health Letter, Rachel and Jacob's relationship suffered especially when he gets angry with her and says, *"Am I in God's stead, who hath withheld from thee the fruit of the womb?"* Rachel couldn't see that even without children, Jacob loved her and would do anything within his power to make her happy. All Rachel could see was every time she turned around Leah was pregnant and popping out child after child like a production line produces product after product. This was her reality and no matter how much she tried her infertility became a bone of contention that negatively impacted her relationship with her beloved, Jacob, and everyone else that she decided was insensitive to her current condition. This reproach was more than Rachel could handle. It was affecting her personally and how she interacted with others. I remember before I got married whenever I went around a certain group of women at Church, they would constantly ask me when I am going to get married. It bothered me so much that I began to avoid them like the plague. I am sure the looks, whispers and hushed conversations had Rachel imagining they were talking about her and her barren condition. They were pitying her, and that more than anything else bothered Rachel. For the first time in her life she was being pitied instead of her pitying someone else.

THE CONCEPTION. Rachel struggled with her barrenness because she wanted so desperately to have children. To give her husband sons that it consumed her entire being and life.

One would have thought she would be happy with her two (2) surrogate sons, but she wasn't. She wanted to experience pregnancy and giving birth to children with Jacob just like Leah, Bilhah and Zilpah. In Genesis 30:22, God answers her prayers and opens her womb. Rachel conceived and bore her first son, **Joseph** whose name means *adding*, and thereby proclaimed that she would have another son (Genesis 30:24). It was then that Rachel realized and acknowledged that "*…God had taken away my reproach.*" The reproach of barrenness with which she was "*…reproached among her neighbors and perhaps by her sister Leah, and indeed it was a general reproach in that day and time…*" (Genesis 30:23; Commentary & Verse meaning – Bible; *www.biblestudytools.com*) In Genesis 30:8 we find Rachel saying, "*…with great wrestling have I wrestled with my sister, and I have prevailed.*" This reiterates my earlier statement that in some ways Rachel and Leah both saw this as a competition with the grand prize being Jacob's love. Rachel became so consumed with giving Jacob sons, like Leah, that she forgot to remember that Jacob loved her to the exclusion of anything and/or everyone else.

Throughout history we find women who believe in their hearts if they have a child(ren) by the man they want it will cause them to stay with them, to love them in the way they needed and/or be committed to them; which isn't the case in most instances. We know that Jacob was committed to Rachel and truly loved her, however, she felt within herself that her place in the family was not cemented if she didn't provide Jacob with children, specifically a male child.

I often wonder if the pressure and stress Rachel was placing upon herself had a role in her barrenness, although I know that God was responsible for her barren condition. In the season God had ordained it to happen, Jehovah-Rapha (the God who heals) spoke into and over Rachel's life, body and situation and opened her womb allowing her to birth Joseph while speaking over her own life that "...*the Lord shall add to me another son.*" (Genesis 30:24) Between the birth of Joseph and the birth of Rachel's second son, Benjamin, the family goes through many transitions. Jacob leaves Laban's home as overseer of his sheep (Genesis 31:14-23); Rachel steals Laban's gods (Genesis 31:30-35); Jacob and Laban enter into a covenant of peace (Genesis 31:43-53); Jacob wrestles with God, and God changes his name to Israel (Genesis 32:24-32; 35:10); Jacob reconciles with Esau and settles in Canaan (Genesis 33:1-19); Dinah the daughter of Jacob is raped (Genesis 34:1-5); Jacob's sons deal deceitfully with Hamar and Shechem (Genesis 34:25-31); Jacob makes an alter to God in Bethel (Genesis 35:1-7); and God speaks the Abrahamic Covenant in and over Jacob and his descendants (Genesis 35:9-15).

In Genesis 35:16-20, we find Rachel travailing as she was in hard labor. As Rachel was birthing her second son with Jacob, she began to realize she was dying and named their son, Benoni, which means the *son of my sorrow*; to which Israel (Jacob) changed his name to **Benjamin** which means *son of my right hand*. Rachel never got to experience the pride in raising the two (2) sons she birthed with the man she loved,

Jacob/Israel. I am certain that because of the close relationship that Rachel had with her handmaid, Bilhah, she was charged with raising Rachel's sons as her own after Rachel's death. This great loss left Israel without the love of his life and evidence of him playing favoritism to the son's she birthed him over all of his other sons.

RACHEL'S TOMB. After Rachel's death she was buried on the way to Ephrath which is Bethlehem. Jacob set a pillar upon her grave that is honored and recognized by both Jews and Arabs today. It is now marked by a small building with a white dome, one (1) mile from Bethlehem and three (3) miles from Jerusalem. In death Rachel has a place of honor that's recognized even today as Rachel's Tomb.

THE CONCLUSION OF THE MATTER: Even though Leah began to step into her own, there was still that place in Leah's heart where she was desperate to be seen as valuable, lovable and wanted by her husband, Jacob. She was searching for something that could not be found from without. According to the *5 Keys to Attracting the Love of Your Life* article, "*…When you are willing to take loving action in your own behalf to bring yourself joy, then you are no longer dependent upon another to do this for you. Your happiness attracts others who are also making themselves happy, and opens the door to a happy, loving relationship.*" How many women throughout time have found themselves growing into the woman she was created, destined and purposed to be only for those old feeling of desperation, rejection, uncertainty and/or fear begin to rear their ugly head(s) and she finds herself doing whatever is necessary to get them to go away. Let's not judge Leah and Rachel too harshly concerning their choice to give their handmaids Zilpah and Bilhah, to Jacob as wives (concubines). Their individual and collective act of desperation is no different than the acts of desperation women make today in having babies in hopes of keeping the man, making him love her or in thinking this will force him to stay. Or even the acts of desperation where women offer their young daughters to their significant others or husbands to keep their marriages intact. Just like in those scenarios, we find Leah acting in desperation to keep the upper hand she believed she has after learning that her sister gave her handmaid, Bilhah, to Jacob as a wife (concubine) to have her children in her stead. It was almost as if Leah felt her position of honor within the family was being threatened and she had to do whatever was necessary to ensure she didn't lose any of the ground she felt she had obtained as being the only wife able to give Jacob children and not just any children but sons.

In everything that we have learned about these four (4) women it has become apparent that each dealt with barrenness in their own lives and allowed that relationship to overshadow any and everything else in their lives. Rachel's story is most tragic of all because she found herself experiencing a life that she never in a million years thought she would ever experience. She allowed her desperation to speak of her true character and the lengths she would go to just to have a child. In the same way that her beautiful body turned on her, she turned on the people she loved and meant the most to her because she did not know how to deal with the fact that she was barren, the upper hand her condition gave her sister in this triangle called a family and in dying before she could really experience the joy of birthing and raising the two (2) sons her beloved Jacob/Israel fathered. Rachel is a representation of how outward beauty does not always mean that there's inner beauty as well. The challenges we see each of these women deal with reminds me that without a foundational relationship with God, learning how to love yourself and learning to effectively deal with disappointment; true happiness can never be found nor experienced in its most altruistic form.

How many women throughout time have experienced what Leah and Rachel went through and how they individually chose to handle their current circumstances and/or situation: by any means necessary while using the tools within their reach. In most cases it's their body and when that didn't seem enough Leah and Rachel, both, used the body of their handmaid or slave that was under her authority, and in no position to refuse. I am sure Leah shared her most personal thoughts and her secrets with Zilpah and over time Zilpah grew sorry for and/or became a willing vessel for Leah to continue to win in the birthing of sons' game she played against her sister, Rachel. It was almost as if she said, "I may not have his love, but I do have his respect and adoration for the six (6) sons I am responsible for birthing." In some strange way, Leah found comfort in this and continued feeling and probably acting superior to her sister, Rachel. I wonder how many times a day Leah reminded Rachel of her barrenness, threw a pregnant Zilpah in Rachel's face and taunted Rachel because in some small way it made her feel somewhat better about herself and her loveless marriage. The continuous taunting and birthing son after son made Rachel more miserable with each passing day, month and year that she wasn't able to conceive and birth a child. The desperation Rachel felt, the anger and resentment she exhibited and tragic end to her story reminds me that true happiness is our own responsibility and it must come from the joy that lives in our hearts and projects outward to the world that we live in and that encounters us.

Nothing else is mentioned of Bilhah after her intimate encounter with Reuben, Jacob's eldest son. However, she is remembered as one (1) of the seven (7) matriarchs in Genesis and to the Israelite nation (1 Chronicles 7:13). Although this is where the story ends for Zilpah and baring children to Jacob as recorded in Genesis, some believe that additional children were born to Zilpah and Jacob that aren't recorded as a part of the 12 tribes of Israel and as heirs to the Abrahamic covenant. Zilpah continued to be Leah's handmaid and Jacob's concubine. It is said that both Bilhah and Zilpah are buried in the Tomb of the Matriarchs in Tiberias, Israel, along with several biblical women: Jochebed, mother of Moses, Zipporah, wife of Moses, Elisheba, wife of Aaron and Abigail, one of King David's wives.

LET'S TALK ABOUT IT: In the lives of these four (4) women: Leah, Bilhah, Zilpah and Rachel, we find an interesting dynamic. A dynamic that shows us how each woman struggled with who they are and their role in the family; specifically, the struggle that Leah and Rachel go through for dominance and a place of honor in the family. Throughout time we have seen women despise other women simply because they either covet or desire the position and/or relationship they witness them having with their significant others. Let me put a caveat here, this very thing happens as a part of the family dynamic when sisters are compared to or pitted against each other for position, acceptance, attention and love. I sometimes wonder what life would have been if Rachel had not died in childbirth but lived a long life. How would Leah have been treated, would she be buried in her place of honor, would Jacob's favoritism towards Rachel and their sons create a different ending to their story and would Reuben have disrespected Jacob and Bilhah's bed? Take a minute and think about your own life and the struggles for position, acceptance, attention and love. Read 1st Peter 4:8 and Hebrews 13:5, how can you utilize the overall message of these two (2) scriptures and apply them to your life?

BIBLE GUIDE QUESTIONS:

1. Why did Leah struggle with self-esteem issues? How did those issues manifest itself in her role as a mother, wife, sister and mistress?

   _____

   _____

   _____

   _____

   _____

2. Why did Rachel decide to use a surrogate? Did her decision to use a surrogate have the same outcome as Sarah's use of a surrogate?

   _____

   _____

   _____

   _____

   _____

3. In what ways did Jacob's acts of favoritism impact his wives and sons? Did those acts divide or create a stronger bond within the family unit?

_____
_____
_____
_____

4. Throughout this section on Comparison Kills, how does depression present itself in the life and actions of the matriarchs?

_____
_____
_____
_____

5. Did the introduction of Bilhah and Zilpah into the family as concubines create greater competition between the

sisters or did it build a stronger bond of love between the sisters? Explain your answer.

CONCLUSION

Throughout history we find individuals who have acted out of desperation. Taking actions and doing things that they feel they have to do because they cannot see another way to get what they want. From Hagar to Rachel, we find the Desperate Housewives of Biblical Proportions acting in desperation for different reasons. Whether it was to reverse the curse of barrenness, to find love, affection and acceptance from their husband or to ensure that their favorite receives the coveted double blessing; each storyline shows that when we look to others for what can only be found from within our self we find ourselves acting in desperation to attain that which we have determined as necessary and desired in our life. Their actions as well as countless women throughout history speak to a personal and intimate relationship with barrenness that presents itself as being desperate in every sense of the word. As you have seen, read and experienced each of the women identified as a matriarch in Genesis and in Jacob's bloodline, their relationship with barrenness resulted in them acting in desperation. A desperation that led each woman to do whatever she deemed necessary to get what she desired while never considering the consequences of her actions and how they would cement the lives, experiences and decisions of an entire nation. They could only see what they could see… only what they desired! I've often said if you are interested in stories like the Desperate Housewives of Biblical Proportions, one of the soap operas within the Bible, then check out the book of Genesis. Everything and then some can be found within its pages. Just as Ecclesiastes 1:9 says, *"The thing that hath been, it is that which shall be; and that which is done is that which shall be done: and there is no new thing under the sun."* All I can say is what these seven (7) women did back then is still taking place today. Although the dates on the calendar have changed, the acts of desperation women commit haven't changed one bit. Their actions, mindset and/or personalities speaks to their relationship with barrenness and how they each individually and collectively gave it permission to play out in their lives and the lives of their children's children visible for any and every one to see.

As we have seen in the storylines from Hagar to Rachel, it is through adversity that the true nature of a person is presented. As I see it, when the fires of difficulty and disappointment are at its highest, the façade that each matriarch wears begins to crack and/or fall off. I would like to say that each matriarch rises from their situation as a phoenix rises from the ashes with strength, courage and faith, and that there is nothing that she cannot accomplish, but I cannot. In each character analysis, we see the matriarch devising and scheming to ensure that whatever they deem as necessary plays out in their life or more correctly to their detriment. In something that I read; I remember it saying that "...*God never intended for Rebekah to sin for the prophecy over Jacob's life to be realized...*" That statement very well could apply to any of these women. What saddens me is that they failed to realize that with God anything can be accomplished as they, like a phoenix, rise out of the ashes and takes flight. The wind beneath their wings teaches them how to soar above the things meant to destroy and distract them while teaching them how to fly to new heights never before known or experienced when faith is the foundation of their choices, decisions, behavior, words and/or actions. More specifically faith instead of fear. In some cases, we can clearly identify when the matriarchs are building a dangerous relationship with fear instead of building a personal relationship with God that develops and increases their faith. If we take a journey through the scriptures, we will see God saying to them individually and collectively, " *Before I formed thee in the belly I knew thee; and before thou camest forth out of the womb I sanctified thee, and I ordained thee...*" (Jeremiah 1:5) and *"For I know the thoughts that I think toward you, saith the Lord, thoughts of peace and not of evil, to give you an expected end."* (Jeremiah 29:11) Although each woman made their individual choices based upon where they were in life, their relationship with them self and their relationship (or the lack thereof) with God, we cannot discount that one (1) of the motivating factors behind their choices is their relationship with fear. Just like with these seven (7) matriarchs, before anyone can live out their divinely assigned purpose, they have to know who they are, whose they are and from whence they've come. Although they played their part in history, each woman walked away with a greater understanding of who she is and what she is capable of doing. Even if it is something that turned out wrong, there was a lesson learned from it. Take a look at Sarah. At no time after Hagar and Ishmael is expelled from the camp, do we see her looking for another surrogate to father additional children with Abraham on her behalf. It does not matter if anyone approves of the actions and/or the role each of these matriarchs played in the birthing of a nation. What is abundantly clear is that in spite of their inadequacies God used each of them in a mighty way for His desire to create a nation unto Himself to be realized. That same thing is available to any woman! If we want to be honest the small part that women throughout history have played has been sewn into the fabric of our society, communities and/or religions. As has been said, the destination isn't the important part; it is the journey taken to get there that molds, strengthens and/or teaches each person what they are made of and capable of doing. Regardless of whether it is seen as good or bad.

Throughout the story of the Desperate Housewives of Biblical Proportions we see the seven (7) matriarchs' relationship with barrenness. In each character analysis, we see the matriarch having a physical and/or Spiritual relationship with barrenness. In Hagar, we see her Spiritual relationship spotlighting her inability to submit and be humble to those who have rule over her and needed in preparation for her to birth a nation. In Sarah, we see her physical relationship in her inability to conceive and her

Spiritual relationship through her emotional immaturity and her inability to visualize and believe in the promises God made to Abraham, and her by default. In Rebekah, we see her physical relationship in her inability to conceive and her Spiritual relationship in her participation in the destructiveness of favoritism and how it birthed dissention, dishonesty and the spirit of entitlement that planted seeds that grew into generational curses that continues to plague the Israelite nation, today. In Leah, we see her Spiritual relationship in her personal, emotional and mental devaluing of herself which leads to feelings of being unlovable and unworthy that she allows to present itself as a competition for Jacob's love. In Bilhah, her Spiritual relationship is through her silent suffering at the hands of those charged with her care and those she grew to love. In Zilpah, we see her Spiritual relationship when she allows her body to be used as a part of Leah's competition with Rachel for Jacob's affection. And, in Rachel, we see her physical relationship in her inability to conceive and her Spiritual relationship show up in the form of jealousy that showcases the ugliness of her personality/character (that's contrary to her outward beauty) and presents as a bad attitude and a nasty disposition.

It is my belief that the person who grows through and comes out of the adversarial experiences these women have encountered when life happens; shows forth the light of love, the experience of going through and how one can overcome with faith, grace, power, strength and courage their relationship with barrenness through the development of the skills and tools needed to divorce their relationship with fear. It is then, through their testimony, they are able to say, "I have gone through the fire and developed into the woman I am today because of my relationship with God (through Jesus Christ), my foundation built upon the word of God and my faith that says I don't smell like the smoke of the fiery furnace encounter I've experienced nor do I look like what I have been through." It is only then that a person can honestly say what these women could not say, 'I have "...*overcame... by the blood of the Lamb, and by the word of* [my] *testimony...*",' (Revelation 12:11a).

Thank you, Jesus, for the blessing of and the opportunity to tell the seven (7) matriarchs of Genesis' story for all the world to see and experience. In their own unique way, each woman made their relationship with barrenness work for them instead of growing out of them. From Hagar to Rachel, I can clearly see how their individual and collective relationship with barrenness has created the platform and/or foundation on which the Israelites have stood on for centuries and continues to stand on today. It literally is the place from which the Christian, Muslim and Jewish religions have sprung forth. All of humanity, in some way, share and/or form, stand on the shoulders of these great women and represent the continuation of their individual and/or collective relationship with barrenness.

What I learned while on this journey, is that each woman's story is woven into the fabric of life that shows up unexpectedly in the lives of women today. If we'd admit it, their stories are a mirror image of ours at different stages and/or seasons during our journey called life. It affords us a rare opportunity to recognize the areas in our individual lives where growth is needed; people are to be released and we take responsibility for our actions and/or behaviors and their corresponding consequences. All while allowing God's love to be the balm of healing that gives Him greater access to our hearts and lives for continued Spiritual growth and development.

In writing this book, I have one (1) desire and purpose for each reader, studier and learner is that God will *"…grant you, according to the riches of his glory, to be strengthened with might by his Spirit in the inner man; *[17]* That Christ may dwell in your hearts by faith; that ye, being rooted and grounded in love, *[18]* May be able to comprehend with all saints what is the breadth, and length, and depth, and height; *[19]* And to know the love of Christ, which passeth knowledge, that ye might be filled with all the fulness of God…"* (Romans 3:16-19), and know that Jesus can *"…do exceeding abundantly above all that we ask or think, according to the power that worketh in us."* (Ephesians 3:20)

BIBLIOGRAPHY

The Change: Medical Problem or Spiritual Passage, by Ellen Besso, www.life.ca/naturallife/0608/spiritual_menopause.htm

Infertility Treatment: An Overview: What causes Female Infertility, http://web.stanford.edu

The only child: everything you need to know, answered by research, https://researchaddict.com/only-child-effects/, December 9, 2018, by Christa Spraggins)

Assyrian tablet reveals ancient marriage contract with surrogacy clause, https://vardags.com/family-law/assyrian-tablet-reveals-ancient-marriage-contract-with-surrogacy-clause, January 3, 2018, by Thea Dunne

5 Keys to Attracting the Love of Your Life, www.huffpost.com, 07/03/2013 | Updated September 2, 2013, by Margaret Paul, PhD

Jewish Women's Archive – Bilhah: Bible, https://jwa.org/encyclopedia/article/bilhah-bible, February 2009, by Tikva Frymer-Kensky

Bilhah | The amazing name Bilhah: meaning and etymology, https://www.abarim-publications.com/Meaning/Bilhah.html#.XzXqdehKjIU,

Old Testament Hebrew Lexical Dictionary – Zilpah – a trickling, https://www.studylight.org/lexicons/hebrew/2153.html

ABOUT THE AUTHOR

Michelle P. Jones is an ordained minister, an Amazon International Bestselling author, business and ministry strategist, and inspirational/motivational speaker. Michelle is the President/CEO of Michelle P. Jones, Inc., a professional services firm, where she specializes in informing, empowering and equipping entrepreneurial creatives in structuring their business/ministry endeavors for success and continued growth. Michelle has self-published two (2) books for national distribution: *Grasping your success: Six steps to Starting an Legitimizing your Business* and *Walking on Water in my Stilettos: How God Strengthened my Faith-walk*, is a contributing author in *As for Me and My House: Stories to help on board households for entrepreneurship*. Michelle is also the executive producer and host of the *Girlz Talk... Real Talk Podcast*, that can be found on all major podcast platforms, where she provides a safe place for women and men to have those difficult yet necessary conversations that have the potential of changing the trajectory of their life while empowering and enabling them to live their truth, their purpose, their life OUT LOUD and in living color. Michelle also is the author of *"Purposeful in Stilettos"* a monthly Blog on the Enhanced DNA Publishing website: *www.EnhancedDNAPublishing.com*.

If you have any questions and/or to obtain additional information, please contact Michelle via email at MzMichellePJones@gmail.com or on her website at http://bit.ly/MichellePJones-Inc.

Enhanced DNA Publishing
DenolaBurton@EnhancedDNA1.com
www.EnhancedDNAPublishing.com

www.ingramcontent.com/pod-product-compliance
Lightning Source LLC
LaVergne TN
LVHW051522070426
835507LV00023B/3244